ONE FOR ALL

ONE FOR ALL

How to Systemize Kindness,
Grow Your Network, and
Support Others Like It's Your Job

MARC C. SHAFFER

ONE FOR ALL
How to Systemize Kindness, Grow Your Network,
and Support Others Like It's Your Job

Copyright © 2025 by Marc Shaffer

All rights reserved. No part of this book may be reproduced, distributed, or transmitted in any form or by any means, including photocopying, recording, or other electronic or mechanical methods, without the written permission from the publisher or author, except as permitted by US copyright law or in the case of brief quotations embodied in a book review.

Disclaimer: Although the publisher and the author have made every effort to ensure that the information in this book was correct at press time, and while this publication is designed to provide accurate information in regard to the subject matter covered, the publisher and the author assume no responsibility for errors, inaccuracies, omissions, or any other inconsistencies herein and hereby disclaim any liability to any party for any loss, damage, or disruption caused by errors or omissions, whether such errors or omissions result from negligence, accident, or any other cause. In addition, the information provided in this book is for educational purposes only and does not constitute financial advice. The author is not responsible for any actions taken based on the information provided. Readers should consult with a professional advisor before making any financial decisions. The opinions expressed in this book are solely those of the author and do not reflect the opinions of any organization or entity.

Interior Layout and Design by Stephanie Anderson
Book Cover Design by Abigael Elliott

ISBNs:
979-8-89165-320-7 *Paperback*
979-8-89165-322-1 *Hardback*
979-8-89165-321-4 *E-book*

Published by:
Streamline Books
Kansas City, MO
https://shareyourstory.com

To my wife and kids—
You are my heart, my purpose, and my greatest joy.
This book is for you and because of you.
To anyone who believes that kindness is a strength—
May this serve as a reminder that your efforts matter
and your impact is always greater than you think.

A portion of the proceeds from the sale of this book will be donated with intention to meaningful causes. Information can be found at searcyfinancial.com/OneForAll.

Contents

Introduction. i
Picturing Your Legacy. iii
The Relationship Business. v
What to Expect in This Book vii

STEP ONE
Decide What You Want to Be Remembered For 1
Build Your Personal Brand. 5
Leverage the Power of Mentorship. 6
Find Your People. 13
Find Your Purpose. 15
Seek Diversity. 17
Learn When to Say Yes and When to Say No. 19
When to Ask for Help: Life Coaching 21
The Real Meaning of Wealth 24
Bringing It All Together 27
ACTION STEP
Create Your Connection Sheet. 28

STEP TWO
Discover How You Can Help 31
Hunting in the Same Forest. 33
Relationships Beyond Referrals 34

Joining the Rotary Club 37
Referrals and Introductions. 40
Make a Bigger Pie 41
Strategies for Efficient Networking 45
The FORD Method 47
Leveraging AI Without Losing the Human Touch. 53
The Other Side of the Coin: The Assessment Trap 55
ACTION STEP
Stock Your Connection Toolbox 57

STEP THREE
Connect, Human to Human 59
Build Your Database 61
Essential Ingredients. 63
Techniques for Active Listening. 68
When to Say No 72
Room to Grow. 74
ACTION STEP
Up Your Communication Game. 76

STEP FOUR
Follow Up and Follow Through 79
Essential Principles for Following Up 81
ACTION STEP
Personalize Your Communication Timeline 95

STEP FIVE
Nurture the Relationship 97
Methods to Maintain Accountability and Support Systems . 99
How and What to Delegate. 102
Show Up Intentionally on Social Media 104
Try Communication That Transcends Business 106
Know When to Let a Relationship Go. 108

Your Biggest Relationship............................... 111
Putting It All Together 114
ACTION STEP
Turn Your Connection Piece into Shareable Content 115

Conclusion 119
Acknowledgments 121
Recommended Reading................................123
About the Author 127

Introduction

Hand it out in slices and it comes back in loaves.
—IRISH PROVERB

We often hear about the value of random acts of kindness. Do you know what's better than that? Kindness as a way of being, both in life and at work, that creates the kind of world you want to live in.

How we get there is the opposite of random. (Although, don't get me wrong: any act of kindness, random or not, is worthwhile.) A more sustainable path is one that's systemized, one that's repeatable.

Walking this path can benefit you professionally and help you live a more fulfilling life. It takes practice and intention, but it's worth the effort tenfold. And don't worry: it's not rocket science. While a lot of these concepts are relatable in the financial industry (and examples will reflect that), the principles of living and leading One for All can be applied to many industries. By the time we're done here, you'll be empowered with a simple, step-by-step system that shows you the way.

Picturing Your Legacy

I believe in the power of living One for All, which is my way of saying "paying it forward." For me, that looks like facilitating connections to people and opportunities. If someone wants to grab coffee with me and talk about something they're working on or something they'd like to accomplish, I'll take them up on that without fail. If I can help them, I will. If I can't, I probably know someone who can. Does this practice grow my network, which comes in handy in my role in the financial planning industry? Sure it does. Is that the reason I do it? No, it's not.

My vocation and educational background intersect with my desire to serve. At Kansas State University, I earned a degree in Family Studies and Human Services, allowing me to look at financial planning through the lens of relationships, families, and how people feel about their futures. The focus and motto for the College of Health and Human Sciences at KSU is "in a world focused on things, we focus first on *people*" (emphasis added). I couldn't love that more. That's stuck with me for a while, and I'm glad that my major is rooted in this specific college instead of only business because it focuses more on humans, relationships, money scripts, financial therapy, financial planning, and so on, which continues to match my preference for who we work with.

At my financial planning firm, we help our clients go through an exercise to write their vision for their life. We get to know them and ask them questions that have nothing to do with money. For instance, as George Kinder says, "If you were to go to a doctor and find out you had five years to live, what would you do differently? If you went to the doctor and found you had twenty-four hours to live, what regrets would you have? The idea is to get them to realize any of us could die tomorrow, so why not live the life you want today?"

Too many people get caught up in money and what's happening next week, completely losing sight of their legacy in a hundred years. Simon Sinek says if you don't start with the end in mind, you don't get to take action on it.

Through doing these exercises, I've found most of us want the same things: family, love, and to be remembered as a good person, partner, friend, parent, sibling, and so on. You get the picture.

Money is a tool to help us reach those larger goals; the bigger rewards are found in the relationships we create along the way, which will become our legacy.

The Relationship Business

It's true that every business owner is, in some way, in the relationship business. Whether you sell to customers or other vendors, those are relationships. But this book is not only for people who need referrals for a black-and-white reason at work. Why? Because it's also true that relationships and our overall sense of community have deteriorated since the pandemic. During lockdowns, familial ties largely strengthened, but connections with friends, local communities, and broader social groups weakened. This shift was driven by the necessity of isolation, which, unlike other crises that encourage people to come together for support, forced individuals to stay apart to avoid spreading the virus. As a result, the collective resilience and altruism typically seen after natural disasters were muted, replaced by prolonged uncertainty and loneliness. Even after restrictions eased, these social disruptions had lasting effects, making rebuilding networks and fostering kindness more crucial than ever.[1]

My point is that all of us need connections to progress, and those connections always come back around. By focusing on the

---

[1] Ashwini Ashokkumar and James W. Pennebaker, "Social media conversations reveal large psychological shifts caused by COVID-19's onset across U.S. cities," *Science Advances* 7, no. 39 (2021), https://pmc.ncbi.nlm.nih.gov/articles/PMC8457655/

connections rather than the sales, you can tap into a life or purpose and service. When I say helping others comes back around, I mean it's a virtuous cycle. The more you do it, the more positive reinforcement you get, and the more you'll want to keep helping. Through building that habit, you help the world and yourself in a win-win way that becomes second nature. As you experience more good results, you'll want to do more. Good energy begets good energy, spiraling up. If you're not careful, the opposite is true as well: negativity begets negativity. The good news is that we have a choice.

I choose the helping route, the positive route, the One for All route. If you picked up this book, odds are you do too.

What to Expect in This Book

We need each other; nobody does anything alone, really. In the business world, we need referral partnerships and networking. In our personal lives, we also need advocates who can help and support us when we face a challenge. Whether it's a personal or professional advisory board, find your people, whoever they are. Then, help them. And let them help you. The circle goes round and round. That's what One for All means to me: expansive kindness, expansive connection, expansive growth in a way that is systemized. No guesswork, no randomness.

Whether you're just starting out or a seasoned connector looking to deepen your practice, you can benefit from the five steps to living One for All that we'll explore together in this book:

1. Decide (or double down on) what you want to be remembered for.
2. Discover how you can help.
3. Connect, human to human.
4. Follow up and follow through proactively and systematically.
5. Nurture the relationship and help one another grow.

Even though the point of our time together is to empower you to make outward connections with other people in the world, Steps One and Two require you to look inward first, getting to know your passions, your values, and the kinds of people you want to bring into your circle. If you take your time there, in Steps Three, Four, and Five, you are set up for success on the external front.

I'm a realist, and at the end of the day, you can choose how much of the five-step system you want to implement in your life. I choose to do all of it because it works for me and is highly process-driven. If some aspects feel like too much for you, that's OK. Tailor it to your needs and style. Adopting a system and consistently following it, whatever you decide to take or leave, will make a significant difference in your bid to connect with and serve others.

At the beginning of this book, I shared an Irish proverb with you: "Hand it out in slices and it comes back in loaves." Besides being a beautiful reminder of the power of generosity and reciprocity, there's more to these words, in my eyes: "Coming back in loaves" doesn't have to mean financial rewards. It can also mean the following:

- **Emotional support and connection.** When you consistently offer kindness, encouragement, or a listening ear to others, you create deeper, more meaningful relationships. Over time, those same people will be there for you when you need support, often in ways you never expected.
- **Community and social impact.** Volunteering your time, sharing knowledge, or simply being a good neighbor fosters a sense of belonging and connection. What starts as small acts, like helping an elderly neighbor with groceries or mentoring a young professional, can grow into a thriving, supportive community that lifts everyone up.

- **Personal growth and fulfillment.** Generosity isn't just about others; it also transforms you. When you give your time, energy, or talents freely, you cultivate a sense of purpose, gratitude, and joy. That fulfillment often far outweighs anything you "get back" in a material sense.
- **Health and well-being.** Science shows that acts of kindness improve mental and physical health. Giving slices of positivity and living One for All, whether through small gestures, compliments, or words of encouragement, creates a ripple effect that fosters overall well-being, both for the giver and the receiver.
- **Creativity and inspiration.** Sharing ideas, collaborating, or mentoring others doesn't deplete your creative energy; it expands it. Many artists, writers, and entrepreneurs find that by sharing their insights or encouraging others, they receive inspiration and fresh ideas in return, often leading to unexpected breakthroughs.
- **Love and kindness in daily life.** A simple smile, holding the door for someone, or showing patience in difficult situations often leads to a more positive environment around you. The goodwill you spread often circles back in unexpected ways—maybe not from the same person but from the universe in general.

This proverb isn't just about getting back more than you give; it's about the abundance that generosity creates in all aspects of life. I advise my team to focus on the right activities and putting as much good out into the world as possible, no matter what loaves come back (or what loaves don't), and I live my life that way, too.

When you transform these five steps to living One for All into habits and continually repeat them, success will come to you naturally and authentically. In the meantime, you'll find more fulfillment and purpose through connection and relationships than you ever imagined possible.

I know because I'm living proof.

Let's get started.

STEP ONE

Decide What You Want to Be Remembered For

Working hard for something we don't care about is called stress; working hard for something we love is called passion.
—SIMON SINEK

In high school, I worked at a sandwich shop where I used to sell drugs to the security guards and the girls at the nearby pretzel stand, covertly slipping the goods between fountain cups. (Bet you didn't think I was going to start with that one, huh?)

I wasn't cut out for that kind of life. I was only the money person, getting a small return for a whole lot of risk. I was young and dumb back then. Maybe it was an early attempt at entrepreneurship, but I certainly wasn't helping people in a way I'd want to be remembered for. My stint in that business didn't last long, and I'm not proud of what I did. I only share it with you now because it's such a juxtaposition to what I do today and what I believe: that we should act in accordance with how we want to be remembered. And, if my story proves anything, it's never too late to start or change course.

Before I left for college, I definitely dabbled in what some might call the "laid-back" lifestyle—let's just say there was a lot of couch-sitting, snack-eating, and not much motivation to get out and explore. My friends seemed less interested in meeting new people, and I started to realize that this routine wasn't leading anywhere I wanted to go. So when I packed my bags for K-State, I also packed up those old habits and left them behind.

Determined to embrace the full college experience, I decided to do what every social butterfly in college does: crack open a beer (responsibly, of course). But more than just swapping vices, this transition was about finding connection. I became more interested in getting to know people, discovering mutual interests, and saying yes to new experiences. That shift in mindset ended up steering me toward a major that revolved around what I was growing to love most: building relationships. Funny how one decision can change everything.

One of my favorite quotes is "The difference between who you are today and who you are in ten years can be found in the books you read and the people you meet." That is a big reason why you can find a recommended reading list at the end of this book, as that's certainly true in my life. A long time ago, someone told me not to put relationships after work but to fit them *into my work*. Even when I worked constantly and didn't feel like I had time for anything else, I still made time to make connections because I made connections at my job. In this way, I've been intentional with who and what I've surrounded myself with, and it's helped me transform. Today, I know what I want to be remembered for and what my purpose is: to do good work, and to help others.

For example, in the realm of mentorship and connection, I've learned that, sometimes, the most profound impacts come from unexpected places. I maintain an open-door policy for anyone seeking guidance—a practice that keeps my calendar full but my life richer for it. One such meeting began with an email from a young woman exploring a career in financial planning. Though she lived in a different city and came from a different background, her interest in the profession resonated with my passion for being a catalyst for positive change.

While there wasn't a position available on our team, I invited her to shadow me in Kansas City, sharing insights into the day-to-day reality of financial planning. I connected her with K-State University's Financial Planning Program, and our correspondence continued for six months—until tragedy struck. The sudden loss of her husband changed everything, including her career aspirations.

In the wake of this devastating loss, our relationship shifted. The trust built through those months of mentoring created a foundation of connection that extended beyond career guidance. Though she never entered the financial planning profession, she became a bridge to others who needed financial guidance, including her parents, who became one of our firm's largest clients.

This experience taught me a profound lesson about serving without expectation. What began as mentoring a potential future competitor transformed into a treasured relationship that enriched both our lives in unexpected ways. The connections forged through genuine service—to her, her family, and the friends who became clients—remind me that opportunity often arrives wearing an unfamiliar face. We need only keep our doors and our hearts open to recognize it.

Note that an open-door policy isn't just about welcoming mentees; it extends to collaborating with others in the same industry. At the end of the day, we're all working toward the same goal: helping our clients (and patients, neighbors, and friends) thrive. Learning from peers has been invaluable to me, which is why I joined my local Financial Planning Association Chapter early in my career. That decision led to leadership opportunities, fresh insights, and even changes in how we operate as a firm. Our founder always said, "We're on the cutting edge, not the bleeding edge," meaning we constantly evolve to improve—but in a smart, strategic way. By staying open to conversations with fellow professionals, we ensure that growth never stops.

Think in abundance: the more slices, the more loaves. Infinitely.

Build Your Personal Brand

Step One of building your process of systemizing kindness, growing your network, and supporting others like it's your job is deciding what you want to be remembered for. That requires what I call developing a personal brand. There's a difference between people who have a job, go to work, and head home at five versus the people serving in their vocation, which is their passion or career calling. A vocation is more than a job; it becomes who you are.

Whether you have an idea of your personal brand or you're still discovering and building it, the following pillars will guide and inform your next steps.

Leverage the Power of Mentorship

Finding a mentor can further your purpose, allowing you to dream bigger than you thought possible. All of my mentors have believed in everything I've stretched for. Without some of them helping me along the way, I might have gotten complacent.

Some mentors enter your life like gentle waves, slowly reshaping your shoreline of thought. Others crash in like tsunamis, fundamentally altering your landscape. Mic Johnson has been both for me over the past decade, serving as a steady presence while periodically delivering profound perspective shifts that have transformed my approach to both business and life.

As the founder of Introducing Awesome, a peer networking group for small business owners, Mic created more than just a professional network. He built a community where genuine connection transcends business cards and elevator pitches. His philosophy of "swimming in the deep end" isn't just a catchphrase. It's his authentic approach to human connection, diving beneath surface-level interactions to forge meaningful relationships.

Mic's own journey shapes his perspective. Having lost his father in his early twenties, he embraces a powerful motto: "Carpe Diem the Shit Out of This Life." This isn't just about seizing the day. It's about grabbing hold of life's essence and refusing to let go. His commitment to this philosophy shows in his unwavering availability; despite running a demanding meeting-planning business, he's never once failed to be there when I've needed guidance.

Our quarterly meetings have become anchors in my chaotic schedule, providing space for reflection and growth. Through these conversations, Mic has consistently challenged my definition of success, teaching me that true wealth isn't measured in dollars but in moments. "There is nowhere else you need to be than spending time with your family," he reminded me during my struggle to adjust to fatherhood, when my productivity-driven mindset clashed with the demands of parenthood.

This mentorship has been a masterclass in presence and perspective. While I still grapple with my tendency to chase productivity at the expense of peace—a work in progress, as Mic would say—his guidance has helped me understand that life's richness lies not just in achieving goals but in savoring the journey toward them. Through Mic's mentorship, I've learned that sometimes the most productive thing you can do is simply be present, learning to appreciate the roses rather than rushing past them in pursuit of the next milestone.

Bill Meredith is another core mentor of mine. He entered my life during my freshman year at K-State, where he served as associate dean of Human Ecology before becoming a professor of Leadership Studies, a role that perfectly matched his gift for nurturing future leaders. Our connection began through Silver Key, an honor society where he served as a mentor, but it was during the organization of a homeless awareness sleep-out in front of the student union that our relationship truly took root.

From those early days, Bill has been an unwavering voice of possibility in my life. His consistent message, woven through every conversation, has been simple yet profound: I am capable of achieving whatever I set my mind to. This wasn't empty encouragement; it was a challenge to dream bigger than myself, backed by his visible pride in every step I took forward.

Life has a way of deepening mentorship through shared experiences. When Bill lost his wife to ovarian cancer and MS shortly after my graduation, it sparked my involvement in the Bike MS Ride, an event I've now completed eight times. Rather than letting loss define him, Bill channeled his energy into nurturing younger generations, mentoring fraternity members in both Delta Chi and Beta. These connections he fostered have enriched my life in unexpected ways, leading to lifelong friendships, business relationships, and a broader network of inspired individuals.

Perhaps Bill's most persistent gift to me was his relentless invitation to explore the world. Year after year, he invited me to China, and year after year, I declined with the familiar excuses of insufficient time and money. When I finally accepted in 2012, traveling to Hong Kong and China with a small group of K-Staters, it broke down the mental barriers I had built around international travel. Since then, Bill's influence has led me to summit Mount Everest in Nepal, trek through Namibia and South Africa, explore the ancient kingdom of Bhutan, traverse the landscapes of Iceland, and adventure through Patagonia, Chile, Argentina, and Peru.

Looking back, I realize that Bill didn't just mentor me. He expanded my world, literally and figuratively. His persistent belief in my capabilities, coupled with his gentle push to step outside my comfort zone, has transformed me from a K-State freshman into a global citizen. Every passport stamp, every mountain conquered, and every new friendship formed across continents stands as a testament to Bill's impact on my life. I'm a better person because of Bill, not just for what he taught me but also for the doors he convinced me I was capable of walking through.

I've had many other mentors like Mic and Bill who have been

transformational on my journey. Without my life coach, Kay, for example, I may never have met my beautiful wife. You'll hear that story in this book—and those of many other impactful people who have helped me become who I am and who I am still becoming today. The caveat is important: I have not "outgrown" the need for mentors. Far from it. Whether your personal brand is already deeply rooted or you're still planting seeds, mentorship can provide the nourishment necessary for growth.

Get Out of Your Comfort Zone

Getting out of your comfort zone isn't just about proving you can do something difficult; it's about expanding what you believe is possible. Every time you push beyond what feels comfortable, you redefine your limits, and what once seemed intimidating starts to feel routine.

I experienced this firsthand during my first Century Ride on the Bike MS Ride. Before that day, riding a hundred miles in one stretch felt impossible. But as I pedaled through the exhaustion, I realized that the only person I was racing was myself—my own doubts, my own limits. Crossing that finish line changed my mindset completely. Suddenly, riding a hundred miles wasn't some unthinkable feat; it was just something I could do. And just like in life, once you push past one barrier, you start wondering, *What else am I capable of?*

A true thought partner, like Bill in this case, will push you and make you feel uncomfortable when necessary. Some people shut down in the face of that kind of feedback, but I invite you to be open to everything. You might feel taken aback by something a mentor says, but if you've chosen thoughtfully, they mean well and have your best interests at heart.

This muscle of taking feedback is one a mentor can truly help you strengthen. For instance, I hired a COO and told her I don't want people to feel like they have to work long hours just because I do. So, she set a policy that I can't send emails to people after 5 p.m. or before 7 a.m. If I'm being honest, at first, it annoyed me because I wanted the team to know that *I* was working at 9:00 p.m., not because I expected *them* to but because that's when I catch up after being in meetings all day. However, she saw the impact in a different light, and I needed to be open to it. I hired her for a reason. It doesn't make sense to listen to a viewpoint only when it aligns with ours.

The lesson here is to keep an open mind and to make sure you've chosen a good, honest, and trustworthy mentor. Otherwise, it doesn't make sense to open yourself up to their advice. They also need to be available to meet with you regularly, one one-on-one.

Who you meet and spend time with becomes who you are, so be careful about the people you select to connect with, employing a level of discernment. I want to be remembered for saying yes, but it's also important to protect your time. For me, it's always a work in progress.

Be Open to Mentoring Others

If you've got your personal brand dialed in and know how to use it, then *you* should become a mentor. I'm currently mentoring a young man in my industry, which is highly rewarding and also eye-opening. I'm realizing that I'm becoming the old-school person, and his generation has different ideas about what's worth striving for and how much effort to exert. Sometimes, it feels like I don't have time to mentor or be mentored, but those meetings always get me thinking in a different way and push me to continue evolving.

The journey is never done, so even when you have a great amount to teach, there's still more learning to do. I learn from the man I'm mentoring, even as he learns from me.

You use your brain in a different way when you're teaching versus learning. Teaching requires you to explain what has become second nature to you when you're in your element, which clarifies your abilities further. That's a major benefit to serving as a mentor. On a more personal level, mentoring has given me the confidence to get through anything in life. It brings deep satisfaction and joy to be part of what helps someone achieve change.

Make the Time

It can feel overwhelming to add something else to your schedule, like mentoring, when you're already busy. One of my strategies is to get everything out of my head and onto either paper or a digital system with reminders of what I need to do. If you get things out of your head, they won't take up space in your mind, continually recurring and distracting you. Your brain doesn't function as clearly if you try to store important commitments in your memory. They'll swirl around in the background while you try to focus on other things, like a computer with too many programs using up RAM. Instead, write down what you need to do, put it in a calendar, or take it one step further.

Investing in automation and technology isn't just about efficiency; it's about reclaiming time for what matters most. I recently started using Calendly, though I hesitated at first because I wanted to "control my schedule." What I learned was that I could still maintain full control by setting boundaries, adding buffers between meetings, and limiting how soon someone could book time with me. Even better, I automated the email reminders I was manually sending every day. Now, instead of trading ten emails to set up a meeting, someone can check my real-time availability and book a time that works for both of us, whether it's a client meeting, coffee chat, happy hour, or lunch. If plans change, they can easily reschedule through a reminder link, again eliminating the endless email back and forth. While scheduling meetings is essential, the method for doing so shouldn't be a time drain. Sometimes, the right tech doesn't just simplify a process; it improves the experience for everyone involved. And the best part? Updates like this provide value that far exceeds the cost, making them an easy decision for anyone looking to maximize their time.

Today, my calendar includes my top priorities. If I've listed something for three weeks and still haven't gotten to it, then maybe it's not the priority I thought it was. Either way, I've written it down and gained a clear head so I can move forward. Anything I think of that I want action on, I put on my calendar.

We've only got so much time. Best to use it wisely.

Find Your People

Whether you have already established your personal brand or are just getting started, one fact remains: we need each other. Finding people who support you and whom you can support in return is the point of life, let alone the point of this book.

For the introverted among us, this might feel easier said than done. If this is you, I recommend starting with the path of least resistance: do something you like to do and meet others who share that interest, which can provide both personal and professional benefits. Along the way, you might find opportunities to mentor others or discover an organization you can become a part of. Start with what fills your cup, and then go from there.

By showing who you are, you're more likely to find your people—people with similar interests, values, and needs that intersect with what you have to offer personally or professionally. For instance, one of the employees I mentor plays piano. He and a client began talking about music because the client saw a piano in his background on Zoom, and it turned out the client's child was attending a well-regarded music conservatory. The employee ultimately attended the child's concert, which fostered a new point of personal connection between them, even though the conversation started about business.

The more you put yourself in the position of finding your people and helping others as you strive to live One for All, the more you make new connections. You never know how your actions will come back around to you, but if you consistently serve others, something's always coming back around. That's why I tell my team to focus on the activity, not the result. The results come when they're supposed to. You can't force results, just like you can't force sales. Everything has its own timeline. If you just focus on activity, you'll reap the positive byproducts.

If you feel ready to find or become a mentor, consider how your personal brand and vision can extend through the connections that you'll make when you start to actively find your people. For instance, in my experience, board service has been hugely beneficial. Other people get more involved in their industry in a way that promotes their purpose rather than directly engaging in business development. Both options allow you to meet peers, learn from them, and share your knowledge.

"Networking" doesn't have to mean approaching people in a transactional, sales-y way. If you do what you love and care about, sales can naturally follow without being the focus. If someone needs help, why shouldn't you be the one to offer it? If you have a talent but don't give back to others, you're not fully serving your larger purpose.

Find Your Purpose

Goals and vision are incredibly important in life, like a North Star. What if I told you that the true magic lies not just in reaching that star but in discovering the constellation of possibilities that surrounds it?

Consider for a moment walking down a long hallway. Ahead lies the door you've always imagined walking through: your predetermined destination. Many of us walk down this hallway with tunnel vision, our eyes locked firmly on that single door. But lining this hallway are countless other doors, each slightly ajar, each offering its own unique opportunity. These aren't detours or distractions; they're the universe's way of conspiring in your favor, as Paulo Coelho so eloquently reminds us in one of my favorite books, *The Alchemist*.

Think about the most significant moments in your life. How many were meticulously planned? How many instead came from embracing an unexpected opportunity, following an unplanned path, or learning from what appeared at first to be a setback? These moments weren't accidents; they were teaching you lessons and guiding you toward where you needed to be.

This doesn't mean abandoning our goals or drifting aimlessly. Instead, it means holding our aspirations with open hands instead of clenched fists. When we embrace this truth, our journey becomes less about reaching a specific destination and more about growing into the person we're meant to become, which, if you ask me, is the ultimate purpose.

Seek Diversity

As you work on finding your people, take care that not all of them look, think, or live exactly like you. Diversity isn't just about race and ethnicity; it also includes differences in age, professional backgrounds (profit and nonprofit), thought leadership, sexual identity, and life experiences.

I live in Johnson County, Kansas, and my wife and I are both white, though we think differently from each other politically. Unfortunately, Rotary® (which I'll tell you more about later) isn't particularly diverse, so I made it a point to join the Centurions Leadership Program as well. That experience introduced me to a broader pool of leaders from different generations, industries, and backgrounds, which has widened my perspective in ways I wouldn't have gained otherwise.

Connecting with a diverse group of people helps you expand your horizons, think more creatively, and develop a deeper understanding of the world around you. And, personally, I've found that the best way to grow is to surround myself with people who challenge my perspectives—I'm always ready to listen and learn.

It's true that you are the accumulation of people you meet, so be thoughtful when it comes to whom you surround yourself with. Otherwise, you might live in an echo chamber and not have a full sense of what is possible personally or professionally. As part of your self-reflection, every once in a while, look around the room you're in and do a gut check: Who's in this room? Whose voice is being heard? If there's a lack of diversity, how can you seek that out?

Learn When to Say Yes and When to Say No

When it comes to building your personal brand, balance is key. In general, I advise you to say yes to things, especially if you're just getting started on your connection journey. Put it in the universe that you want to help others, and see what comes back to you.

At the same time, be careful not to become overcommitted. Sometimes, you don't know what you like until you've tried it, so all you do is what you *think* you like. There's a whole world out there that you don't yet know. For example, I didn't travel internationally until I was in my late twenties, and then I loved it and wished I'd tried it earlier. Be open to experiences, from adventures to charity work, as you're discovering who you are; try to keep all of your eggs out of one basket.

Finding balance is a process. I'll be honest: I'm still learning how to get it right myself, so I don't have the perfect answer for you. There's a Warren Buffett quote I keep in mind: "The difference between successful people and really successful people is that really successful people say no to almost everything." To me, that means there's a careful balance of saying yes to discovering new horizons but not letting it take over your whole life.

Your life flows from the priorities you set and being great and whatever drives your passion. Say yes to the right things and no to what will derail you from your course, but also leave room to say yes to new experiences so that you keep learning and growing. Keep experimenting and pushing yourself outside your comfort zone. When you find what lights you up, be sure to lean into that and center it in your priorities. If you want to try a charity group, excellent—but don't say yes to a five-year term as president unless you know it fully aligns with your purpose. Otherwise, you might end up resenting the commitment.

When to Ask for Help: Life Coaching

There was a time in my life about a decade ago when, from the outside, people thought I had it all. Though I seemed like a successful guy, there was something missing on the inside. One symptom of that lack was that I dated the wrong people for a while and felt generally like something was missing. I knew I needed a professional to give me advice and help me become a well-rounded person.

It can be hard to be vulnerable and ask for help, but I'd hit a wall and knew I needed an outside perspective. I felt a sense of safety in working with my life coach; it's more confidential and impartial than talking to your mom or a friend. This is important because if you're trying to maintain a persona to the outside world, it can feel threatening to let people in on what's bothering you. In my case, even when I tried, my friends didn't take me seriously, saying things like, "Come on, it's not that bad. You're successful and happy." On one level, it was true that I had a good life, but I wanted help to achieve more, including meeting a partner and having a family.

When I went on my search for a life coach, I didn't want someone who would simply hype me up and tell me how great I was; I wanted feedback that would lead me to grow and change. I wanted someone to help me find the answer to a question I kept struggling with: If I was doing as great as people thought, why did I feel so empty inside? I found the help I needed in a coach named Kay.

I spent an hour every week doing one-on-one coaching and opening up to her. Living One for All by being of service to others became my answer to filling that emptiness. Now, I do group coaching, which started out with ten people and has grown to fifty people via Zoom. It has become an accountability partner group for everything from professional concerns to personal challenges, such as fighting cancer or going through a divorce. We're all trying to help each other and benefit from Kay's life coaching.

As my coach, Kay's full-time job was to make me uncomfortable, and I *liked* that. She was great at helping me identify ways to work toward more balance and reprioritize my time. Staying present with my discomfort led to huge successes in various areas of my life. My coach helped me see that I could be even more successful financially, but that wasn't what I wanted. I wanted to take care of my mental health and find a spouse, which meant making some tradeoffs.

She told me, "Slow down to speed up. You're going too fast all the time." If I said yes to everything, I couldn't slow down to figure out what I wanted. If I continued that pattern over a lifetime, I'd lose. She taught me that I needed to find more quiet moments to connect with my own authenticity, staying in touch with who I really am.

Before I had that guidance, I just kept chasing more money. I figured I'd fill the hole I was feeling by working harder and getting richer. Without balance, that path only amplified the sense of emptiness. Instead of facing the problem, I just leaned into what I was good at professionally without getting any closer to fulfillment.

Kay called me out for that behavior, telling me, "You can do that, but just know that's not where you want to go based on what you've just said is important to you."

Whether or not you decide to hire a life coach, it's important to take an unflinching inventory of where you are versus where you want to be and what your values are versus how you're actually living right now. The gaps between the ideal and the reality are where you need to focus your energy on changing course.

Wherever you're starting from, whether you know what you want to be remembered for or are still figuring it out, there's a level of discomfort inherent in determining the next step. The good news is stepping into that discomfort builds more connections.

The Real Meaning of Wealth: Balancing What Matters Most

For years, I thought wealth was all about financial success: working harder, making more, and stacking up wins in my career. And while financial security is undoubtedly important, I've learned that chasing money alone can leave you feeling empty. There's a reason we see high achievers who seem to "have it all" but still feel unfulfilled. That's because true wealth isn't just about money; it's about balance across different areas of life.

Sahil Bloom captures this concept perfectly in his book, *The 5 Types of Wealth*. He challenges the traditional notion that financial wealth is the only kind that matters. Instead, he introduces five distinct types of wealth:[2]

1. **Time Wealth**—Having control over your schedule and how you spend your days.
2. **Social Wealth**—Building deep relationships and a strong network.
3. **Physical Wealth**—Maintaining health and well-being to live a long, active life.

---

[2] Sahil Bloom, *The 5 Types of Wealth* (Random House Publishing Group, 2025).

4. **Mental Wealth**—Finding purpose, peace, and personal growth.
5. **Financial Wealth**—Achieving financial security and freedom.

Reading his framework helped me articulate something I had been experiencing in my own life: I wasn't truly wealthy when I was only focused on financial success. I had to learn, sometimes the hard way, that real wealth comes from balance. And I didn't come to that realization alone. With the help of my life coach, I began to understand that fulfillment wasn't going to come from simply making more money. It had to come from a more holistic approach to life.

Take time wealth, for example. Early in my career, I would say yes to too many things. More meetings, more projects, more commitments. I told myself I was "hustling," but in reality, I was just busy. The problem? I had no real control over my time, and I was constantly exhausted. It wasn't until I invested in tools that I realized automation and boundaries could give me more time for the things that actually mattered.

Social wealth is another big one. We all know the saying, "It's not what you know; it's who you know." But it's not just about knowing people. It's about building real relationships. I've seen firsthand how surrounding yourself with a diverse group of people broadens your perspective and challenges you to grow.

And then there's physical and mental wealth, two areas that are easy to neglect when chasing success. It wasn't until I pushed myself through my first Century Ride (a hundred miles in a single day) that I truly understood the connection between physical and mental endurance. That ride wasn't just about finishing; it was about proving to myself that I could push beyond my perceived limits. The same applies to mental wealth: if you're not taking care of your mind, everything else in life suffers. Working with a life coach taught me that slowing down, prioritizing mental clarity, and making space for what really matters are just as valuable as financial success—if not more.

One of the biggest myths people believe is that you can only have two out of three at any given time: time, wealth, or health. We've all heard it before: When you're young, you have time and health but no money. In midlife, you have money and health but no time. And later in life, you finally have money and time, but your health may be declining. But what if that isn't true? What if balance across all areas is actually possible? My coach helped me see that I didn't have to sacrifice one type of wealth for another; I just had to be intentional about where I invested my energy. By focusing on *all* five types of wealth, I could avoid falling into that limiting belief and instead build a life where time, wealth, and health work together rather than against each other.

The biggest takeaway from all of this? Wealth is about more than money; it's about balance. You can have all the financial success in the world, but if you're burned out, lonely, or in poor health, what's the point? The goal isn't just to build financial wealth. It's to create a life where all five types of wealth thrive together.

Bringing It All Together

Let's take a step back: Where are you truly wealthy? And where are you lacking? The sooner you recognize the gaps, the sooner you can start making intentional shifts toward a more fulfilling, well-rounded life.

I want to be remembered as a loving husband and father who has the energy to invest in people and causes he cares about. Although I can't say yes to everything in reality, I want people to think of me as someone who always makes time for what's important. I also have specific interests that make up my personal brand, such as international travel, loving K-State and bleeding purple, and contributing to my community through various involvement. All of these interests and focus points are components of my personal brand, themes I come back to again and again. These themes also take center stage on my Connection Sheet, a robust resource I developed for when I meet new people that's specifically designed to facilitate connections and grow and support my network.

ACTION STEP
Create Your Connection Sheet

You picked up this book because you know your life has more potential than you're currently reaping. When I was in the same place, creating a Connection Sheet helped me set my goals in motion and gave me a jumping-off point when making new connections. Use mine as inspiration to create your own.

BRINGING IT ALL TOGETHER

CREATING CONNECTIONS

I believe in making connections to better my community, my network and myself. Below, you'll find some information about the people I like to meet and help, and I would love to know the same about you. Who do you want to meet? What type of people do you enjoy? Who do you want to help? Let's connect!

Personal Introductions

I enjoy meeting people who have an interest in or enjoy:
- International Travel
- Personal Development and Leadership
- Bleed Purple and Love K-State - I'm a member of the Wabash Cannonball Steering Committee and Serve as Director of Partnership for the Annual Event
- Physical Activity: Hiking, Biking, Running
- Community Involvement, Giving Back, Volunteering, Networking, Serving on Boards & Non-Profit Consulting. Some of my involvement includes Rotary International - Overland Park South Rotary Club, Centurions, Top Gun Kansas City, Big Brothers Big Sisters, Growing Futures Early Education Center, Leukemia & Lymphoma Society, MS Society
- Craft Beer and Wine

Professional Introductions

My firm works as a team, but clients are paired with their Lead Advisor based on the best fit for their situation. We also bring our own professional network contacts to our firm to add value for our clients. I feel a connection in working with and networking with the following types of people:
- Successful Couples Building Toward Their Future
- Young Families or Couples Looking to Start a Family - I have personal experience with fertility treatment and my wife and I are very open about our success with IVF
- People New to KC Looking to Engage in the Community
- Sales Professionals Who Value Business Coaching
- People Who Under Promise and Over Deliver
- Other Successful Financial Planners
  - I often recruit for the Financial Planning Association but also want to meet others who could be a good addition to our team. We hire when it benefits our team so it is good to know our competitors.
- People in Transition
  - Moving to a new job, a new location, looking for a change in some aspect of life
  - I enjoy connecting people to the resources they need, in all areas of work and life

In my first book, One for All, I reveal the counterintuitive truth I've discovered throughout my career: the most successful people aren't those who focus on themselves, but those who systematically support others.

Let's Connect Online

	Searcy Financial Services	Allos Investment
My Bio	Website	Advisors Website
My Personal Facebook	Facebook Page	Facebook Page
My LinkedIn	LinkedIn	LinkedIn
My X or @MarcCShaffer	X/Instagram or @SearcyFinancial	X/Instagram or @AllosAdvisors

 MARC@SEARCYFINANCIAL.COM | 913.814.3800

STEP TWO
Discover How You Can Help

They don't teach you this at Harvard Business School . . . it's all about people.
—MARK H. MCCORMACK

The other day, I had lunch with a younger gentleman whom I mentor regularly. As we caught up, he started telling me about how his business purchase in Wichita was opening up new opportunities he hadn't expected, opportunities that were setting him up for even greater success. I was thrilled to hear how things were coming together for him, but what really surprised me was what came next.

He told me that the entire business development and purchase in Wichita traced back to *one* introduction I had made for him *several years ago.* That connection, seemingly small at the time, turned out to be the catalyst for changing the trajectory of his business. If no other introduction I'd ever made had an impact, *this* one was more than worth it.

I so enjoy hearing stories like this—about how introductions, suggestions, and encouragement spark unexpected success. And while I had no idea that introducing him to a friend in Wichita would turn into something so significant, I was more than happy to hear about it. This is why I always keep promptings in mind—those gut feelings, small nudges, or moments of inspiration that push us to reach out, connect, or offer support.

Sometimes, the prompting leads me to tell someone I care about them. Other times, it's sending a handwritten note, posting something kind on their Facebook page, inviting them to grab coffee or break bread, or simply introducing them to a friend who might be able to help them in some way. None of these actions require much time or effort, but they can lead to incredible results down the road.

You can have your own stories like this one. Once you've decided what you'd like to be remembered for, it's time to discover how you can help by identifying and leveraging your unique skills and networks to help others. Remember: the overall goal of living One for All is to systemize kindness, which will result in positive outcomes for you personally and likely professionally as well. But those outcomes should be pleasant byproducts rather than the primary focus. As we explore all the ways you can help others, repeat after me: service without expectation.

The key is to act without expectation and simply sit back and enjoy the excitement of what could come from it. Some connections will take root and flourish into something life-changing, while others may not, but that's not the point. The point is to consistently put good energy into the world, to systemize kindness, and to trust that, somewhere along the way, the right moments will align in ways you could never predict.

This chapter is about discovering how you can leverage your unique skills, network, and opportunities to help others. And sometimes, the best way to start is by simply listening to those quiet nudges that tell you to reach out because you never know what they might lead to.

Hunting in the Same Forest

Don't overcomplicate the art of discovering how you can help. I recommend you start by finding the people to whom you can add immediate value. Do you know people at church? Are you highly connected through your alumni network? What professional organizations do you belong to (or could you join)? When you turn an intentional lens on the people you know, you'll likely realize there are far more people and opportunities than you originally thought.

The easiest way to start is through your profession, connecting with what I think of as people who "hunt in the same forest." The low-hanging fruit is whatever you do at your nine-to-five job. Because I work in finance personally, I can most easily help people find accountants, estate planners, and professionals who touch the financial planning process. Those referrals offer an easy way for me to make a positive impact, and they're more relationship-based than transactional.

Ask yourself: What groups of people can you help based on where and with whom you're connected professionally? You might be pleasantly surprised by how many potential answers—and, by default, potential points of service and connection—this one simple question can yield.

Relationships Beyond Referrals

Sometimes, the most pivotal moments in life start with something as simple as a business card. I still have the one Mike Searcy handed me at that Financial Planning Association® Chapter meeting at Indian Hills Country Club. As I watched him drive away in his two-seater sports car that day, I couldn't have known how thoroughly this man would shape my professional future.

Our first interaction was classic Mike: direct and challenging. "Why would I hire you? You don't have any experience," he quipped. A year later, after cutting my teeth at an independent RIA in St. Louis and accumulating an alphabet soup of certifications, I called him back. That conversation began a mentorship that would eventually lead to a partnership with Searcy Financial Services, the firm that now provides my family's livelihood.

Mike had an uncanny ability to prevent complacency. "Fat and happy" was never an option under his guidance. He consistently pushed me to stretch beyond my comfort zone, opening doors I hadn't even noticed were there. But perhaps more importantly, he taught me to value my own expertise. In moments when I was tempted to discount the importance of financial planning, Mike would remind me of the real impact our work had on people's lives.

His wisdom extended far beyond portfolio management and financial strategies. When I hesitated to take my first international trip, citing the familiar excuses of insufficient time and money, Mike offered the perspective that would change my trajectory: "Say that enough times in life, and you won't see very many places." He insisted that time and money would materialize if I prioritized the opportunity. Taking that first trip as a "broke kid in my twenties" proved him right; it not only broadened my horizons but created new opportunities that funded future adventures.

Mike's influence led me to Rotary, though not directly to his own Leawood club. Choosing to forge my own path, I found a home club that helped me develop leadership skills and pushed me to become more extroverted in my business development approach. The irony wasn't lost on me when, years later, I found myself traveling to Portugal with leaders from Mike's very own Rotary Club.

His mentorship in financial prudence, living well below my means, and consistently investing in the future laid the groundwork for sustainable success without the burden of excessive debt. When he offered me a partnership in the firm, I promised to be his "best investment yet." Our partnership expanded possibilities for both of us, proving that good mentorship creates mutual growth.

Now, as Mike enjoys his well-deserved retirement in Naples, Florida, I look forward to raising a glass with him to celebrate our shared journey. While I'll forever be in his debt, I know he'd prefer I pay it forward, creating opportunities for others just as he did for me.

When he was at the helm, Mike prioritized doing business with referral partners. I came to him and said I wanted *my* referral partners to be people I develop friendships with and would want to have a beer with on a Friday night. (In other words, real connection.) Mike has always supported that approach. For instance, I found out my realtor went through IVF, just like my wife and I did. She walked me through that process, and we met for coffee just to hang out and talk about her kids.

I'm aware that my method might reflect generational differences and the increasing emphasis on aligning with a sense of purpose; it's likely true that in the past, people were more likely to find someone to get something done without regard to the relationship piece. Neither way is right or wrong, but my approach aligns with my priorities, values, and overall happiness today. Whatever approach you choose, make sure you have that alignment too.

Joining the Rotary Club

For me, joining the Rotary Club was a way to get involved with potential mentors who were older business leaders. I didn't want to live under my boss's shadow, so I joined a Rotary Club chapter different from his. It took a unique approach in that it gave young people the opportunity to step up and do whatever they wanted to. If we had an idea, they'd empower us to figure it out and run with it. If someone had an aspiration to be president, they took it seriously. By contrast, other clubs wanted people to pay their dues for ten years before trying anything.

Because this Rotary chapter had weekly meetings, there was an opportunity to get to know people better than if it only convened once a month. I knew I wanted to get involved in nonprofit work, and Rotary would give me exposure to a wide variety of nonprofits. At least twice a month, a nonprofit guest speaker would present to us, and the members also included nonprofit leaders. Rotary showed me a range of options that I might want to get more engaged with, giving me the information I needed to uncover a calling.

I threw my hat in the ring to chair an event called Jazz in the Woods, a volunteer-led three-day free music concert focusing on jazz music connected to Kansas City's history. The event attracted thirty thousand people and raised money for charity. That role was a stretch for me because I didn't even like speaking in front of groups. However, it ended up being a blast, and our biggest fundraising year brought in $150,000.

There was a lot to do. I am a detail-oriented person, but I like the people part of getting everybody motivated around a central goal and managing the process. When I was younger, if you'd asked me whether I'd chair an event where I didn't know what the hell I was doing, I would've said no. However, by taking a chance, saying yes, and getting out of my comfort zone, I developed friendships, learned that people are talented in other areas that complement my weaknesses, and figured out how to use those talents. That lesson has been carried through my company and volunteering to this day. Essentially, I experienced Dan Sullivan's principle that success is not about "how" but rather "who."

Rotary Relationships

Rotary has provided me with friends all over the globe. Not only are there approximately a hundred members in the Overland Park South Club, but also I've met members in other area clubs and in other parts of the country and the world. Through my role as president, I went to Portugal with Rotary to attend the international convention, which takes place in a different location every year. I loved Portugal; everyone was so welcoming. People extended hospitality in their homes, which feels rare among Americans, who love their downtime. I traveled there with two other club members, and then we spent two weeks traveling through Spain for fun.

I've made so many connections, and I stay in touch with people who retire and move away. One of them took me under his wing when I joined at age twenty-five. In other clubs, people expect members to belong for at least fifteen years and be in their sixties before they take on leadership roles, and this guy fit that bill. However, he wanted to mentor me, in part because he knew I was there to make business connections and become a leader in my company and in the community. He saw something in me that I didn't yet have the confidence to see in myself. He pushed me forward and believed in me to figure out what I needed to do, providing accountability and opening doors along the way.

It was useful to me to have someone who could provide an outside perspective on my company, who could bounce ideas with me, and who came from a different generation. He'd been very successful in business and had traveled the world for his work back in the day. Now, he lives in Florida, and his daughter has become one of my clients. Mostly, I value our friendship. He watched me date some of the wrong people and then meet my wife. Even though he's moved away, he's still there to check on me and ensure I'm living up to the standards that I told him were important to me.

That relationship is just one of many that has been hugely fulfilling for me personally while also inadvertently bolstering my referral network. When you build relationships based on mutual trust, they can benefit you in myriad ways. Authentic, genuine connections lead people to want to support each other. I've made many of those connections through Rotary, but you could make them anywhere and in any industry.

Referrals and Introductions

Referrals and introductions offer a resource to help people with what they need. As you expand your connections, you'll probably know someone who knows someone who can assist with just about anything. At first, though, you might not know anyone. In that case, find a person who is where you want to be or a group that is making a positive impact, and connect with them.

At this point, I have a robust contact list. If someone asks me for a referral, I probably know ten people who either fit the bill or could connect me to the person who does. You don't need to know everyone personally, but I encourage you to cultivate the skill of finding the right people when needed. When someone asks me if I have a particular kind of contact, sometimes I'll say, "No, but I'll find one."

When I do make a referral, I tell people I want to know how it goes; if it's good, I'll keep sending people, and if it's not, I'll find someone new. That follow-up is important because if you take good care of people, it feeds your pipeline. If you don't follow through, then you're doing more harm than good by providing bad service. (I'll talk more about this in Step Four.) The primary focus is not passing business back and forth but rather strengthening relationships. Do that, and the rest takes care of itself. That's the whole story.

Make a Bigger Pie

I recently took a class with a coach named Zach Arend, and we completed an assessment called the Energy Leadership Index, which divides results into six mentalities. One of them is "everybody wins:" the pie gets bigger, or it's not worth it. Another one is "If I win, somebody loses." I don't think that because I don't believe in real losing. Even a setback is a lesson. Zach explained that the goal is to recognize winning and losing as illusions. Take a higher-level perspective instead of getting caught up in every little advance and obstacle. That's an attitude to which I aspire.

I've always followed this philosophy and believed that if done right, the pie gets bigger for everyone. Too many people operate from a mindset of scarcity, where one person's gain must come at another's expense. But in reality, when people work together, share knowledge, and remove unnecessary barriers, *everyone* benefits.

At Searcy Financial Services, we've built our compensation structure around this philosophy. Our team members are paid based on firm revenue rather than individual performance alone. While not everyone is an owner receiving profit distributions—nor do they take on the downside risk of fluctuating revenue—*everyone* is encouraged to think like an owner. There's no scenario where one person can do well while the rest of the team struggles. We're all invested in making the pie bigger.

As CFO, my focus in recent years has been identifying new revenue opportunities, improving operational efficiencies, and eliminating unnecessary expenses. One thing the team noticed was that I was putting in more hours than I should have. The more time I spent on administrative work, the less time I had to focus on CFO responsibilities that could generate more revenue for the firm. They recognized that if I could focus my energy where it mattered most, on strategy and growth, it would increase revenue for *everyone*.

That's why we're now in the process of hiring an executive assistant. While on the surface this role may not seem as important as others, the truth is that their contribution will be vital. By freeing up my time, this new hire could create more than enough additional revenue to more than justify their salary, expanding the pie for the entire team.

At first, hiring for this position may feel like *taking a step backward*, an added expense without immediate payoff. But sometimes, you have to take three steps back to move ten steps forward. Investing in the right people or the right infrastructure may feel like a temporary setback, but in the long run, it positions you for greater success.

This is just one example of how shifting away from a scarcity mindset leads to *growth* rather than competition. And while this example is from my own business, the same principle applies in many other areas of life.

Here are other ways to make the pie bigger:

- **Nonprofit and community growth.** Many nonprofits view each other as competitors, fighting for the same donor base. But when organizations collaborate by sharing resources, applying for grants together, and cross-promoting events, they often secure larger funding and serve *more* people than they could have alone. A rising tide lifts all boats. Art That Blows: Rockstars for Band of Angels in Kansas City is a shining example of this. Band of Angels is a phenomenal nonprofit founded by my friend, the owner of Meyer Music. Some people have instruments in their closets from twenty years ago or that are broken; he partners with Big Brothers Big Sisters of Kansas City and fixes these instruments, making sure young musicians have access they otherwise may not have had. If some of the instruments are too old, he turns them into works of art, and the Art That Blows fundraiser was born. This is a clear case of two organizations with overlapping priorities coming together and making magic (and, in this case, maybe even a little music) together.

- **Professional networking and business development.** It's easy to think that making introductions will mean "giving away" opportunities, but the opposite is true. When two professionals in complementary industries, like a financial planner and an estate attorney, form a referral relationship, *both* grow. They create better client experiences, generate more business, and build a stronger network.
- **Industry growth through knowledge sharing.** Some professionals hoard information, thinking it gives them a competitive edge. But those who share insights, whether by mentoring, speaking at conferences, or training others, help elevate the entire industry. The result? More innovation, greater demand for skilled professionals, and ultimately, *more* opportunities for everyone, including the original business that shared its expertise.
- **Investing in employee growth.** Companies sometimes hesitate to invest in employees out of fear they'll take their new skills elsewhere. But in reality, when businesses support career development through activities like tuition reimbursement,

leadership training, or internal mentorship, employee satisfaction and retention increase. A stronger, more capable team leads to higher productivity, better reputation, and ultimately, more growth for the company.
- **Entrepreneurship and local economy growth.** Too often, small business owners see each other as competitors rather than allies. But in strong local economies, businesses work together by offering referrals, supporting local suppliers, and co-hosting community events. This attracts more customers, strengthens the business district, and increases economic opportunities for *everyone*.
- **Coaching and mentorship.** Successful professionals don't succeed in isolation. They get there through the guidance of others. That's why great leaders mentor and develop the next generation, even when there's no immediate benefit. The success of a mentee often leads to *new* business, partnerships, and unexpected opportunities years down the line.

At the core of all of this is a simple truth: when we stop focusing on what we might lose and start focusing on what we can create, we all win. The scarcity mindset, or believing that success is a zero-sum game, limits what's possible. The abundance mindset, or believing that success multiplies when shared, unlocks potential we didn't even know existed.

Strategies for Efficient Networking

If the idea of discovering how (and who) you can help feels scary or tricky, I encourage you to find comfort in the fact that you *don't* have to talk to everyone. Find one person to start. If you're feeling shy or overwhelmed, pretend to be Sherlock Holmes for a second. If I walk into a room and feel uncomfortable, I look for someone else with a Rotary symbol on their lapel. Automatically, we have a point of connection.

This is simply one illustration of the larger point: there are ways to learn about people before you talk to them. Is that person over there in the corner proudly wearing clothes displaying the logo of your alma mater or favorite sports team? That's an invitation to open a conversation. Broadly, I look for those clues in an open room to find a point of entry for one-on-one connections regarding a common interest.

If you're drawing a blank about how to find a connection regarding a particular professional need, LinkedIn offers a great place to start. If you're interested in a particular charity, reach out to the membership chair or someone on the board. If you're trying to connect through Rotary, the sergeant of arms is in charge of making introductions. Churches may have similar positions as well. If you find an organization that you think does good work that you're interested in, call or email and ask who is in charge of partnerships.

When you're looking for mentorship, find someone who is where you want to be in your profession. Ask if you can learn from them. Most older people take those requests as a compliment, and they'll sit down with you even if they don't know you. In Kansas City, my experience is there's an open-door policy; if you ask someone to have coffee, there's a 95 percent chance they'll say yes. The culture may vary in other regions, but in general, people appreciate having a way to share their expertise and help others. Don't be scared to ask.

The FORD Method

There's a saying that "nobody cares how much you know until they know how much you care." If you meet people without an agenda and simply focus on learning who they are and where they're coming from, you have the best chance of developing a long-term and mutually supportive connection. Because we're all about systemizing and efficiency, a quick way to find common ground with potential connections is to use the acronym FORD: family, occupation, recreation, dreams.

Family

People tend to prioritize their families and enjoy talking about them. I take that fact a step further than just asking a new connection about their family; I make note of particular information people share with me and then follow up on it to demonstrate I care (more on this in Step Four).

For instance, maybe a client tells me about their first grandchild. I'll then ask what the baby's name is and put a reminder in my calendar to check in on how the baby is doing. In this way, I can deepen my relationship with that person and show I'm paying attention, rather than just saying, "That's nice," in the moment and never bringing it up again. Using what you learn about people and setting yourself reminders to follow up is an example of what I mean by systematizing kindness. It comes from a genuine place while also adding systems to help you follow through.

Occupation

I'm always looking for ways to help others increase their success within their occupation. I benefit because I enjoy meeting people who are passionate about their occupation and want to be around people who love what they do. Generally, I've found that these are the same people who want to figure out how they can make themselves better and do better for their clients.

Sometimes, I find there are gender differences in how people talk about their goals; men may be more inclined to talk about paid work, while women center their families. When I'm using my system, I make sure to read the room. There are also people who don't feel particularly attached to their day job, but their board work or other volunteerism is their true calling. When I meet with them, we focus on their nonprofit passions rather than growing their primary career.

When I meet new people, including clients, I listen for the areas of growth that will align with their sense of purpose. I take notes and am always looking for the next action I could take to help them progress or pay it forward.

Recreation

We all have particular recreational habits that we enjoy, and asking about what lights someone up outside of the office is an easy entry point into a conversation. Everyone has *some* point of connection with you, likely; you just need to figure out what it is by becoming very interested. For example, if someone also went to my alma mater, we could talk about our favorite memories or a bar nearby. As Dale Carnegie put it, "You can make more friends in two months by becoming interested in other people than you can in two years by trying to get other people interested in you."

Dreams

As you seek connection with others in pursuit of finding out how you can help and living One for All, try to determine where people see themselves in five years, personally and professionally. Talking about dreams is vulnerable. By showing curiosity about a person's life, you can figure out whether they're content with where they are or feel excited about where they're going. I like to connect with people who are trying to make themselves better and make positive changes in their communities. When I ask about dreams, I can often find alignment with another person on those issues and am happy to help them with those goals.

When meeting people for the first time, I try to keep this quote in mind from Stephen R. Covey's *The 7 Habits of Highly Effective People*: "Most people do not listen with the intent to understand; they listen with the intent to reply."

It's easy to fall into the trap of listening just long enough to formulate a response or jump in with your own story. But real connection happens when you listen to hear, not just to reply. When I meet someone new, I try to focus on understanding who they are, what they care about, and what's truly important to them, not just what I can say next.

That shift in mindset makes all the difference. Instead of just exchanging surface-level pleasantries, I walk away with real insights into their passions, challenges, and what drives them. And more often than not, that deeper understanding leads to stronger relationships, meaningful introductions, and opportunities to help in ways I wouldn't have recognized if I were only half-listening.

I've found that when I share *why* I'm passionate about something, it makes it real for people—it's no longer just a title or a role but a part of my story. It also builds trust, especially when there's a shared experience. That's why when I tell people that I joined the board of Growing Futures Early Education Center, I don't just say it was a great organization—I tell them why it mattered to me personally.

I joined for two reasons:

1. To support a longtime friend who was serving as the executive director and working to deepen the organization's impact on the community.
2. To give back to kids because, at the time, I wasn't sure if I was going to have my own.

That second reason often surprises people. And sometimes they'll ask me about it—or, more often, I just keep talking about it anyway. That's when I open up about my own journey—about how, for a long time, I wasn't sure if I'd ever find the right person. I was worried I'd missed my chance, and when I finally met my wife, we faced another challenge: fertility struggles.

Our journey led us to out-of-state IVF treatments, three difficult retrievals, two successful transfers, and countless days spent in Denver, all during a pandemic. It was one of the hardest things we've ever been through, but it made us stronger. It deepened our appreciation for our kids and reinforced how much we wanted to be parents. Now, my wife and I are open books—we share our story freely because we know how isolating the fertility journey can be, and we want to be resources for anyone going through something similar.

Whether or not the person I'm talking to has had a similar experience, sharing this part of my life tells them more about who *I* am as a person, including the following:

- I believe in supporting my friends and their passions, just as I hope they'd support mine.
- I try to give back in meaningful ways, especially when I see a need I can help fulfill.
- I value family—not just my own, but the importance of family stability for others, which aligns with my work at Growing Futures.
- I believe in being open and vulnerable because real relationships are built on more than just surface-level conversations.

The best part? Opening up about my experiences often encourages others to do the same. I've had countless conversations where someone later tells me, "You know, I wasn't going to bring this up, but . . ." and suddenly, we're talking about something meaningful in their life—whether it's their own struggles, their dreams, or something they're passionate about.

That's the kind of connection that creates trust, and trust is what builds lasting relationships. So whether I'm connecting someone to a nonprofit, a career opportunity, or a personal resource, I try to do it with the same mindset: not just *what* I do, but *why* I do it.

The Practical Side

The information you can gather using the FORD Technique shouldn't just live in your head. To truly systemize your approach to connecting with and supporting others, you need a system. What works for me is storing all of this information in a CRM system. After every meeting, I enter the personal data I want to remember: their birthday, their dog's name, whatever they might have shared. If I think I might take action on something in the future, it ends up in a task with a timeline.

This sort of documentation works for me because my coach, Kay, taught me a long time ago the importance of getting the swirl out of my head and down into a plan. Otherwise, I wouldn't be able to concentrate in the moment because I'd be trying to juggle all the different dates and reminders associated with people I want to remember. Take my word for it: don't use your head as a calendar, or you won't be able to think clearly. We live in a fast-paced, overstimulating world, so it just isn't practical to lean on your memory. You need a system to store this information, or your good intentions will quickly break down.

People are often amazed that I remember so much about their lives because it seems overwhelming. But I'm not remembering it with my mind; I'm remembering it with an external system.

In my industry, we talk about "touches." You have to touch people one hundred times to get their business, whether that's a Facebook post, an email, a call, an event, a blog post, or something else. I find that personalized touches like little notes are much more meaningful and powerful, business or no business. People often tell me they still have a card I sent them because it's based on our individual connection, not a transactional sales email.

Leveraging AI Without Losing the Human Touch

As technology continues to evolve, I've learned to take advantage of AI and note-taking services to help streamline follow-ups and documentation, allowing me to focus on being fully present in my conversations. I recently started using Jump, a note-taking AI that listens to conversations and transforms them into tasks, notes, and even compliance records. Now, I don't necessarily need compliance tracking for networking or personal meetings, but the underlying benefit of AI-assisted listening (assuming the other person is comfortable with it) is that it lets me stay engaged while ensuring that key takeaways, ideas, and action items aren't lost. Instead of mentally juggling what I need to remember, it documents everything more accurately than I ever could.

Even better, Jump doesn't just capture conversations; it summarizes the next steps, allowing me to seamlessly add follow-ups and timelines into my Salesforce CRM. But what I find even more valuable is its ability to search through past meetings, making it easy to find discussions, key points, or commitments I may have forgotten. In fast-paced networking and relationship building, it's impossible to remember every detail from every conversation—but now, instead of second-guessing myself, I can quickly pull up what we talked about and follow up in a way that feels thoughtful and intentional.

Beyond individual meetings, Jump also helps me identify trends in my conversations. By reviewing past discussions, I can recognize bigger-picture themes emerging across my network, whether they be common challenges people are facing, opportunities they're excited about, or recurring takeaways that indicate shifts in my professional community. This insight allows me to be more proactive—whether that's connecting like-minded individuals, providing relevant resources, or stepping up to solve problems before they become urgent.

At the core of this, however, is a fundamental principle: find a system that works for you, one that enhances your ability to connect rather than detracts from it. The goal isn't to replace human connection with technology but to remove the distractions that might prevent you from truly listening, understanding, and engaging with the person in front of you.

The Other Side of the Coin: The Assessment Trap

While systemizing and operationalizing connection is incredibly valuable, take care to approach these activities with an open mind. For example, several years ago, our team began using the Culture Index Survey as a personality assessment tool—not just for hiring but as a way to better understand and serve our financial planning clients. When I took the survey myself, it labeled me a "technical expert." While this wasn't entirely incorrect (I do enjoy diving deep into the technical aspects of financial planning), it came with an unexpected pronouncement: a consultant told our leadership team that I would never succeed at business development.

This assessment could have become a self-fulfilling prophecy, boxing me into a behind-the-scenes role that aligned with my introverted tendencies. Instead, it became a catalyst for transformation. Over the past fifteen years, I've challenged this narrative, pushing beyond the confines of what a personality test suggested I could achieve. The result? Not only have I helped drive significant revenue growth for our firm, but also I've found deep personal and professional satisfaction in proving that introversion and successful business development aren't mutually exclusive.

Today, we still use the personality profiles with our clients, but with a crucial difference. Rather than treating the results as gospel, we use them as conversation starters and opportunities for clients to explain how the assessment either captures or misses aspects of their personality. It's become a tool for deeper understanding rather than a deterministic predictor of potential.

There's a certain irony in how I now share my story with clients who question their own assessment results. The "technical expert" who was never supposed to succeed in business development has become the firm's primary business developer and motivator. It's a reminder that while personality assessments can offer valuable insights, they should never be allowed to place limitations on our potential. Sometimes, the most powerful catalyst for growth is simply refusing to accept others' definitions of what we can achieve.

Even more valuable than the survey itself is the discussion it sparks. The most enlightening moments often come when people disagree with their assessment results. Those conversations uncover hidden strengths, untapped potential, and personal insights that wouldn't have surfaced otherwise. A survey can categorize traits, but self-awareness and growth happen in the moments of questioning, challenging, and redefining what those results mean for us.

ACTION STEP

Stock Your Connection Toolbox

Helping people is much easier when you have a structured system to work from. I suggest building a concise, easy-to-access summary of the people you trust and regularly look for opportunities to help. This makes introductions more strategic and effective, rather than wasting anyone's time.

Create a simple spreadsheet or CRM entry with these details:

- Name
- Title
- Company
- LinkedIn profile
- Company website
- Areas of expertise (or how they can help others)
- Notes on your last interaction

For me, this list includes about seventy-five people—individuals I know, trust, and am actively looking to support when the right opportunity arises. Keeping this list top of mind ensures that when I meet someone new, I can easily scan through it and determine if a valuable introduction makes sense.

STEP THREE

Connect, Human to Human

Be present in all things and thankful for all things.
—MAYA ANGELOU

Sometimes, the most meaningful mentorships emerge from unexpected places. Jeff Pelaccio and I first crossed paths in Mic Johnson's Introducing Awesome peer advisory group, but our true connection didn't spark until after the group disbanded. Despite, or perhaps because of, our twenty-year age gap, we found common ground that transcended generational differences.

While Jeff was known for mentoring fresh college graduates starting their careers, our relationship took a different path. As I was scaling my business and he was reinventing himself during a job transition, we struck upon an idea: monthly meetings to discuss our networking encounters and potential connections. What began as a practical exercise in professional introductions evolved into something far more meaningful.

Jeff's passion for connecting people manifested in his Corporate Couch podcast, which became a catalyst for expanding both our networks. Through his introductions, I gained access to a rich tapestry of professionals across Kansas City, resources that would prove invaluable not just to my business but to my clients and friends as well. His natural talent for promoting people and companies taught me that networking isn't just about growing a contact list; it's about building a community where everyone benefits.

Most recently, Jeff and I decided to make our monthly conversations public in a new podcast series called *The Corporate Couch: It's 5 O'Clock Somewhere*. It's a laid-back, happy-hour-style show (always under thirty minutes) where we riff on business, life, relationships, and everything in between—no scripts, no fluff. It's a chance for others to eavesdrop on the kind of raw, real conversations we've been having for years, and we hope it encourages listeners to think differently about connection, kindness, and showing up.

Our monthly conversations deepened over time, expanding from business connections to impactful book recommendations, family challenges, and professional setbacks. Yet Jeff's gift was finding the silver lining in difficult times and ensuring we celebrated every win, no matter how small. He became more than an accountability partner; he became a model for the kind of mentor I aspire to be.

In Jeff's vision, Kansas City isn't just a metropolitan area; it's a community that can be made smaller, better, and more beneficial for everyone through intentional connections. Our ongoing dialogue continues to center on this mission, proving that mentorship at its best isn't just about personal growth; it's about creating ripples that benefit an entire community.

And it all started with connecting, human to human.

Build Your Database

Connecting, human to human, is a great way to build your database. Today, I get tons of referrals without even looking for them because people know I'm well-connected and want to help. When you're just starting out, you won't be top of mind, so you need to find people through networking, which builds your personal database of the necessary connections.

Start with friends you already have. Tell them you want to grow your network of professionals who can help people, and see if they can recommend a good financial planner, estate planner, accountant, real estate agent, lawyer, or other set of professionals that align with your industry and goals. Explain that you want to get to know more people in a particular space of interest and see if they'd be willing to make introductions.

I always try to live One for All, so whenever I meet with someone, particularly if someone helps me with a request like an introduction, I end the conversation by asking what I can do for them. When you ask that question with sincerity, it opens a dialogue. I find that people reciprocate, too, when I focus on how I can help them. If you spend 90 percent of your time listening and making a conversation about the other person with follow-up questions, then over the long term, they will loop back and want to help you.

Of course, some people aren't interested in paying anything forward or investing in others, and they may not be worth investing in again. If a connection doesn't seem to be amplifying positivity and making the world a better place, consider how you can redirect your energy toward people who are on the same wavelength. As Jim Rohn says, you are the average of the five people you spend the most time with, so choose wisely. There are givers and takers in the world, and I believe in surrounding myself with givers—people who want to help others and who believe in reciprocity. For them, my calendar is open.

Essential Ingredients

I often think about Maya Angelou's famous observation that "people will forget what you said, people will forget what you did, but people will never forget how you made them feel." First and foremost, when it comes time to connect in person, focus on making people feel welcome, safe, comfortable, and respected, above all else. You will have an easier time setting that tone if you also prepare *yourself* to feel comfortable, from how you dress to setting a general purpose for the meeting, without making a hard sell or closing yourself off to other directions the conversation might go. At the end of the day, you might end up talking about business but focus on connecting human to human. Be vulnerable and relatable.

With that foundation in place, let's explore other components of a constructive, in-person connection.

Send Reminders

Before your meeting, send a reminder via email or text. This may seem simple or like a given, but you'd be surprised at the impact. Your system doesn't have to be fancy, as long as you convey the information. Time is the only thing you can't get more of, so I try to make mine productive and show that I respect others' time as well. Sending a reminder communicates that value.

Choose a Neutral Place

Find what I call a "neutral place" off-site, not in your office. Particularly if you're in sales, you want to remove yourself from a business setting that feels like a pitch. I enjoy taking people to my favorite local coffee shop. That way, we can meet as peers rather than convey that I'm bringing someone into my professional space, where there might be a perception that I hold more power. I approach these meetings as not about business, even though they often end up helping my business over the long term. I want the location to center the relationship first. People need to feel comfortable opening up.

In my world, my personal life is my business life. I don't have an email that's just personal or one that's just business. There's interaction between those aspects of my life, and everything flows together. Any relationship could yield personal or business opportunities or both. Whether a given conversation puts money in my pocket or not doesn't matter to me. I focus on connecting people with other individuals and businesses that can help them with whatever they need.

Taking someone to my home coffee shop is great because I know what to expect, and I can make recommendations off the menu. People know who I am when I walk in, which creates a sense of trust. The person I've invited sees that I go there a lot, which opens a dialogue around the fact that I live down the street. (Also, for that reason, my preference is to have them sit with their backs to the wall to avoid my gaze shifting to people who may be walking in. This works for me; find a system that works for you.)

From there, we can talk about where they drove from and start to connect on a more personal level. I don't have any particular goal or strategy for steering the conversation; it's just a nice way to get us talking.

The next time you're setting up a face-to-face meeting, pay extra attention to location neutrality and see if it changes your experience of the interaction.

Dress for Success

Attire is another consideration. I often dress based on the person I'm meeting with that day. Some clients expect you to wear a tie; others find that overly formal. I focus on dressing nicely in a way that makes a good first impression regarding who I am. Your outfit will vary depending on your context and style, but consider whether, for example, shorts would be too informal. Some business owners reach a level of success where they no longer have to dress up, and they wear flip-flops everywhere. I suggest figuring out a way to dress well and still be yourself. Especially when you're first starting out, you don't want what you're wearing to be a mark against you. The pre-meeting interactions and first impression at the meeting itself will set the tone for your relationship.

Respect People's Time

Respecting people's time includes arriving early, being mindful of meeting length, and ending on time. Even if you're getting along great, in my opinion, an hour is long enough for an initial meeting. Initial connections don't tend to have the energy and attention for marathon meetings, especially if you're just getting to know each other. Save the rest for next time. Leave them wanting more when it comes to continuing the conversation rather than wearing them out.

I apply this rule in business as well; our longest client meetings are now ninety minutes, down from two hours. We also offer the option of just forty-five minutes, which many people choose. We can still provide value in that amount of time; we just need to be efficient. I'd rather see someone for a shorter amount of time than have them avoid meeting at all.

Leverage the Power of Attractive Energy

Showing up with a positive attitude is almost more important than showing up at all. The energy you bring into a meeting is contagious. It can spiral up or spiral down. I believe in showing up with what I call attractive energy: the kind that makes people feel lighter, inspired, and more hopeful after spending time with you. That doesn't mean faking it when you're struggling. If you're not feeling well, physically, mentally, or emotionally, treat it like any other illness. Take time to recover and regroup. You can't pour into others if you're running on fumes. Fortify yourself first so that when you do show up, you bring something valuable to the table.

This might mean getting more sleep, going for a walk, calling a trusted friend, reading something uplifting, meditating, journaling, or even doing absolutely nothing for a while. Don't underestimate the power of small resets. When you take care of yourself, you're more likely to show up in a way that uplifts others. The right mindset, not just presence, is what makes a lasting impression.

Be Prepared for One Big Question

Be prepared for the possibility that someone will ask you how they can help *you,* too. A good conversation is, after all, two-sided. Don't fret. Your tip-of-your-tongue request doesn't need to be something you need or want immediately. You could simply share your areas of interest, in case the other person comes across a relevant opportunity down the road. Maybe you're expecting your first child and want their best parenting advice, for example. Of course, go into meetings with the expectation that you're going to focus on the other person and spend your preparation time figuring out how to be of value to them. Then, if they happen to open the door to reciprocating, it's OK to ask for help and resources related to whatever you're going through personally or professionally. There's a beautiful symbiosis to this kind of connection and systematic kindness, and you deserve your part, too.

Techniques for Active Listening

By learning to practice active listening, you'll become better at understanding the unspoken needs of those around you and, to come back to Angelou's powerful quote, make them *feel* cared for and understood. It's possible to go deep into the components of active listening, but for the purposes of this book, we'll focus on some fundamentals to help you get your feet wet:

Know Your Audience

First, know your audience. Based on the purpose of the conversation you intend to have, engage in preparation and research to ensure you have relevant resources at your fingertips, have thought about potential connections to suggest, and have some possible conversational topics and questions teed up—again, all for the purpose of providing service and value, not asking for it.

Be Present

Being present is simple but not easy. In today's world of constant phone alerts and distractions, it's harder than ever to stay grounded in the conversation at hand. Turn off your alerts, and leave your phone off the table if you'll be at all tempted to look at it while the other person is talking. I like to seat people with their backs to a wall so that I'm only looking at them, not getting distracted by anything behind them.

I also prefer not to sit at a bar and talk side to side; I believe conversations should occur face-to-face. There may be some variations to this guidance depending on personal preference, but whatever you decide, choose the kind of meeting that will set you up for the most success and enable you to pay it forward to the person in the best way possible. If your connection *prefers* a walking meeting, great. Part of being present is continuing to be mindful of your audience.

The simple act of being present in a world full of noise represents an act of kindness in itself. When everything's a priority, nothing's a priority. By cutting out distractions and maintaining focus, you can demonstrate to someone that you're attentive to their needs.

Vulnerability Is Key

Vulnerability is key, and it requires some balance between sharing about yourself and not oversharing or stealing the focus from the other person. Over time, you'll learn to read people and get a sense of how deep you can go with them. As you mirror the other person, you'll get a sense of their level of openness to vulnerability.

Everyone's different, but I've learned to err on the side of being vulnerable. Sometimes, I shoot my shot and talk about a more sensitive subject like IVF or politics, which has led to some deeper connection as well as some discomfort. I know what I stand for, and it's OK to disagree as long as we can maintain a dialogue and show curiosity in each other. If someone isn't open to those harder conversations, then they're not the kind of person I want to connect with long term because I am not interested in staying at a surface level. They might be lovely people to know as acquaintances, but they won't become part of my inner circle. Not everyone I meet will become part of my core list of introductions, and that's OK. Out of three hundred people you meet, maybe sixty will make that cut.

Being an independent thinker and thinking critically are skill sets, not mindsets. Even if you're still in the process of forming your own opinions, you can apply those skills in your life. When I weave my values into a conversation, the other person may agree or disagree, but if they're open to discussing, we have a chance to deepen our relationship. Being willing to go toward those more sensitive subjects differentiates me from people who would rather avoid talking about politics or who "agree to disagree" without any further discussion. Whatever makes you stand out can often be used to your advantage. Love it or hate it, people won't forget you.

Be Curious

Being curious fuels helping others. Sometimes, the best answer you can give someone is "I don't know this specific field, but I could help you figure it out or find someone who can." No one knows everything, and that's OK. Don't pretend to know it all. People trust you more when you're transparent about your expertise and what you still have to learn. That's a very different philosophy from "fake it till you make it," but I know from experience that it works. When you don't know something, it's just another opportunity for you to connect with someone who does. It goes back to "who, not how"—if you don't know how to do something, find out who does.

TECHNIQUES FOR ACTIVE LISTENING

One of the most powerful lessons I've learned in building relationships is being open to being led—by the people you meet and the paths they reveal. Sometimes, you set out thinking a conversation will lead in one direction, only to find that the real value was in an unexpected detour. It reminds me of *The Alchemist* by Paulo Coelho (Can you see a pattern here? I told you I loved this book.), where the journey is guided not by rigid plans but by clues, intuition, and the people encountered along the way. I've learned to trust that when someone enters your life, even briefly, there may be something to learn or explore with them—something you didn't see coming. Letting go of control and following those breadcrumbs of connection can lead to opportunities, clarity, or wisdom you never would have found on your own.

When to Say No

When you're starting out and learning how much energy these connection meetings take, don't book five in a day. Spread them out and give yourself some time to recharge in between. You may find that you thrive on networking and gain energy and confidence over time, but give yourself breathing room as you figure out your style.

You'll need to engage in an ongoing process to figure out where best to devote your time and energy, which starts with identifying the right meetings to agree to—and which don't make sense for you. In general, I say yes as much as possible. I think there's good in everybody. At the same time, you need to take care of yourself, your mental health, and your priorities.

If someone wants to meet and you can't make the time without burning yourself out, it's OK to say, "Not right now." Maybe the meeting could be productive, but you need to push it out a couple of months. I've found if I'm on the fence about meeting with someone, it's best to leave the ball in their court as far as following up to schedule when the time comes. If it's important to them, they will find a way. I don't need to babysit them to make sure they get on my calendar.

In general, I get energy from the meetings I have, but it varies depending on the state I'm in. When I went through a harder time with my mental health, something we'll talk about in Step Five, meetings took a lot out of me. I was buying a business and dealing with my parents' cancer, so I didn't have much left to give to my wider network. It was too much—I wasn't eating or sleeping well, and I lost thirty pounds. As a result, I limited my availability to others. Sometimes, you need to recognize the season of life you're in and adjust accordingly. If you're not in a good head space, you won't be as helpful and engaged in the conversation anyway.

When I suggest saying yes to everything, it's with the spirit of casting a wide net and opening yourself to new opportunities, not burning yourself out.

I try to approach every person I meet with curiosity and the assumption that they have something to teach me. That mindset of abundance helps me remember that helping one person doesn't take away from another; it actually grows the pie for everyone. If you're doing it right, your network doesn't become a competition. It becomes a living system of support, generosity, and growth. There's enough to go around, and giving someone else a leg up doesn't mean there's less for you. It means we all move forward together.

Balance is key; before you agree to something new, check in with yourself. Make sure that you're in a place where you can be of service to other people, which first requires taking care of yourself. As a financial planner, I know firsthand that health is wealth. If you don't have your health, nothing else matters.

Room to Grow

It can be scary to approach people and try to build new connections. I get that. But remember: if you don't put yourself out there, the answer is always no. It's a numbers game: the more you try, the more success you'll achieve. Don't make too much of the letdowns. Sometimes, people say no, and that's OK. Don't focus on the results; focus on the activities. Hopefully, people will take the good you do in the right spirit and build on it, but even if they don't, your part is done. You're living up to your own values and creating the opportunity to make the world better. There's just as much satisfaction in giving as receiving.

In moments of hesitation, when doubt creeps in and you start questioning whether you should take that step, make that introduction, meet up with that person, or offer that hand, it helps to remember this:

> "What if I fall?"
> "Oh, but my darling, what if you fly?"
> —ERIN HANSON

Too often, we let fear of failure keep us from making meaningful connections or taking action in ways that could change lives, including our own. But what if, instead of assuming we'll fall, we assume we might soar? What if that one conversation, one introduction, or one moment of generosity sets off a ripple effect of opportunity?

I help people invest, but I also help them make sure that they die using their last dollar to bring them the most joy. There's no special award for dying with the most money in the bank. Your savings balance doesn't get carved in your headstone. If I die with all my money still sitting in an account, I will have missed a lot of opportunities to enjoy life and make a difference—including by giving some of it away. If more people gave to others rather than clinging to their wealth, the world would be a whole lot better.

I encourage you not to focus on whether or not an individual act will go well. Just focus on being in the moment, making your best attempt to act, and then moving on and trying again. Everything you do offers a learning experience, and what matters is the bigger pattern over time.

ACTION STEP
Up Your Communication Game

When it comes to processing Step Three and getting ready to connect in person, think back to the FORD Technique we learned in Step Two and use it as a connection preparation tool for your "real-life" activities. Prepare yourself ahead of time with some FORD-focused check-in questions that will build connection and open doors.

F for Family
Great Questions

- How's your family doing lately?
- What's a recent highlight with your kids (or grandkids)?
- Are you and your partner doing anything fun together soon?
- How are your parents or siblings doing?
- Do you have any family traditions you're looking forward to?
- What's something about your family that makes you proud?

O for Occupation
Great Questions

- What's something exciting going on at work right now?
- What are you learning or working on professionally?

- What's the biggest challenge you're facing in your role?
- If I could introduce you to someone to help with your business or career, who would it be?
- What do you love most about what you do?
- Has anything changed for you professionally over the past year?

R for Recreation
Great Questions

- What do you love doing when you're *not* working?
- Are you planning any trips or vacations soon?
- Have you tried any new hobbies or local experiences lately?
- What's the best thing you've read, watched, or listened to recently?
- What does your ideal Saturday look like?
- Is there anything fun on your bucket list you're working toward?

D for Dreams
Great Questions

- Where do you see yourself in five years?
- What's something you've always wanted to do but haven't started yet?
- Are there any big goals or personal projects you're working toward?
- What legacy do you want to leave behind?
- If time or money weren't a factor, what would you spend your days doing?
- Is there a cause or mission you're passionate about supporting?

STEP FOUR
Follow Up and Follow Through

No one has ever become poor by giving.
—ANNE FRANK

Systematizing kindness and living One for All is, first and foremost, a human process. Connecting with people can be genuine while also being smart and efficient. Having a template for following up and following through removes the sense of overwhelm.

In a world where follow-through often falls through the cracks, I've developed a networking style that some might call unconventional. After every meaningful interaction, whether personal or professional, I send a detailed follow-up email summarizing our conversation, complete with relevant links and resources we discussed. It's my way of delivering immediate value and laying the groundwork for lasting connections.

This process has transformed countless one-time meetings into ongoing dialogues, spawning unexpected friendships and opportunities. The detailed follow-ups serve as bridges, helping to expedite relationships that might otherwise have remained surface-level acquaintances. They're my way of saying, "I heard you, I valued our conversation, and I'm invested in our potential connection."

However, not everyone appreciates this approach. I once received a reply from someone indicating my follow-up email was excessive and unnecessary. Years ago, this response might have made me question my entire process. Instead, it reinforced an important truth: not every style resonates with every person, and that's perfectly fine. The positive experiences I'd accumulated gave me the confidence to stay true to my approach.

Now, I playfully "warn" new connections about my detailed follow-up process. Their surprise isn't in receiving the email—they're expecting that—but in discovering that I actually follow through on every point we discussed. In today's world, where promises often evaporate into good intentions, simply doing what you say you'll do has become a remarkable differentiator.

This consistency in follow-through isn't just about standing out; it's about honoring commitments. A promise, no matter how small, is still a promise. While my comprehensive approach might not be everyone's preferred style, it authentically reflects my commitment to meaningful connection, and that authenticity itself has become one of my most valuable networking tools.

Essential Principles for Following Up

Just like there are best practices for connecting in person, the same is true for following up and following through:

Focus on the Planting

Recently, I've been mentoring a young professional who embodies a common struggle in business development: the fear of appearing "sales-y" or "pushy." His hesitation resonates with many who enter service-oriented professions, where the line between helping others and promoting oneself can feel uncomfortably thin.

In our discussions, I've shared my own journey of understanding that genuine service often requires gentle persistence. Over the years, many clients have thanked me for being the catalyst that prompted them to take action, even when that prompting required a bit of well-intentioned "pushing." This is especially true in financial services, where I've seen the aftermath of poor advice and understand the importance of helping people avoid costly mistakes before they happen.

"Stop thinking of it as sales," I tell him. "Start thinking of it as providing value that people don't yet know they need." It's about recognizing that sometimes the greatest service we can offer is helping others see possibilities they haven't imagined for themselves. The key lies in approaching these conversations with authentic care for others' well-being rather than focusing on immediate results.

I often use the metaphor of planting trees: focus on the activity of planting not on when the forest will appear. Plant enough seeds of genuine service, nurture those relationships with care and attention, and one day, you'll wake up surrounded by a forest of meaningful connections and opportunities to help others. But like any forest, it doesn't materialize overnight; it grows one thoughtful interaction at a time.

This perspective transforms "business development" from a series of transactions into a journey of service. When we focus on creating value rather than closing deals, we build something far more valuable than a client base: we build a community of people whose lives we've genuinely improved.

Incorporate Your Brand

Act on the personal brand you developed or reenergized in Step One. For instance, part of my personal brand is K-State. When I send out cards, I often use purple ink on a customized card with a Wildcat on the back, which feeds into my image as "Mr. K-State." If people are interested in the university based on what we've discussed, I have a range of resources I can share with them, such as the financial planning program and a schedule of the sporting events that I can invite them to. If people aren't K-State alums or fans, we can still bond based on whatever school spirit or love of sports they might have.

Whether you already have your personal brand fully realized or are still figuring it out, ensure that you start incorporating continuity into each of your touchpoints. Keep circling back or alluding to your core values and aspects of your brand. Maybe you don't drink coffee, but you love herbal teas and can highlight the best ones during your meeting. Maybe you don't drink alcohol, but you can arrange a happy hour with mocktails. Maybe it's National Piano Day and you love to play duets with your spouse, so your follow-up note has a musical print on it.

The possibilities are endless. Be proud of who you are and showcase your strengths.

Don't Force It

If people appreciate you for helping them, allow yourself to take in that appreciation. If they become a referral partner and part of your inner circle, great. That will happen naturally, or it won't. You don't need to force anything. The people who organically become part of your inner circle are relationships you can cultivate with more care and intention. You might stay in touch with others more casually, such as by sending them your newsletter.

Keep feeding relationships that work mutually. Not everybody's going to be your best friend, which is fine, but you can continue cultivating relationships and seeing where they go. Sometimes, that means you need to get vulnerable and be proactive about reaching out, even if the other person doesn't respond the first time.

Stay curious about people, even if the relationship doesn't unfold on your timeline. Just because someone isn't ready to engage today doesn't mean they won't be next month or even next year. Don't take it personally. We all have different seasons. Stay open, be consistent, and leave the door cracked open. When you show up as someone who's thoughtful and generous without demanding anything in return, people remember—and often circle back when the timing is right.

Over time, I've also learned that detailed follow-ups packed with links, attachments, and resources can sometimes trigger spam filters or get blocked by email servers. That's why I've developed a habit of sending a short second email right after my main follow-up, with a subject line like: "One more email . . . " The idea is similar to clicking a reaction on a social media post. It doesn't do much tangibly, but it lets you know you've been heard and seen.

Here's what I typically say in that message:

> *I realize that the attachments and links in my email below may have caused it not to go through, so please confirm receipt of both this email and the one below I sent a few minutes ago.*
>
> *If there is anything else I can be doing to help you at this time, please let me know.*
>
> *If you have any questions or need additional information, please do not hesitate to give me a call.*

This small act has saved me countless missed connections. It's a great way to double down on reliability without overwhelming the recipient—and it subtly reminds them that I care enough to make sure they got the information.

Leverage the Power of a Personal Note

In a digital age where communication often feels automated and impersonal, there's enduring power in the simple act of sending a handwritten note. After every initial meeting, without exception, I write a "great-to-meet-you" note. While the core message might echo similar themes, like expressing appreciation for their time, acknowledging their background, and exploring potential ways to help each other, each note represents a genuine moment of connection.

This practice led to an unexpected win with a prospect referred by my life coach. After our initial meeting, where they expressed interest in our financial planning services while noting they were interviewing other providers, I followed my usual protocol: connecting on LinkedIn for professional updates and Facebook for personal insights. Through these social connections, I discovered they had contracted COVID-19 shortly after our meeting.

Instead of pursuing our scheduled follow-up, I shifted gears and sent a simple Get Well Soon card, not a business development tactic, just a human response to someone facing illness. Two weeks later, I learned through our mutual connection that they had chosen to work with our team. Their reason wasn't about our technical expertise or service offerings; it was because we were the only firm that had shown we cared about them as a person, not just a potential client.

This experience reinforces a fundamental truth in relationship building: people don't care how much you know until they know how much you care. The personal note wasn't a strategy; it was an expression of genuine concern. In an era of automated responses and digital efficiency, sometimes the most powerful connection comes from the simple act of putting pen to paper and showing you're thinking of someone beyond the business context.

There are endless reasons to send a personal note, some obvious, others delightfully unexpected. The classics include birthdays, graduations, sympathy during loss, and celebrations like engagements or new jobs. But the most meaningful notes often come in the in-between moments: after a tough week, when someone is facing uncertainty, or just because they came to mind.

Other great times to reach out include when someone shares a big goal on social media, finishes a major project at work, volunteers for something impactful, takes a leap of faith in their personal life, or even shares a vulnerability. Notes don't have to be reserved for milestones; they can be used to acknowledge resilience, courage, effort, or presence.

Remember: the note doesn't need to be long or poetic. It just needs to be sincere. A quick card that says, "You've been on my mind," or "I saw what you did—amazing work," can leave a lasting impression. In a world where people are used to likes and emojis, a handwritten message says something louder: I see you. You matter.

As my volume of personal notes increased, I found myself searching for a way to keep the quality high while staying consistent. That's when I discovered SendOutCards, thanks to a thoughtful introduction from Brenda Perkins, a senior manager and affiliate with the company. I'll admit, I was skeptical at first—how could something that wasn't handwritten still feel personal?

Then Brenda started sending me cards: thoughtful, customized notes with pictures from my travels, inside jokes, and even my LinkedIn photo mocked up like a news feature. They weren't just impressive; they were meaningful keepsakes. I realized this platform wasn't replacing sincerity; it was amplifying it.

Now, with an unlimited plan and a reminder on my screen to send ten to fifteen cards a week, I use SendOutCards to follow up, celebrate wins, offer support, or just say, "I'm thinking of you." Whether it's a card with sea salt caramels, a thank-you after coffee, or a birthday brownie, these little gestures make a big impact.

Organize Your Inbox Strategically with Rules

In my industry, we live and die by email. There are hundreds every day. To keep them sorted and prioritized in a way that doesn't overwhelm me, I create email rules. How granular you get with your rules depends on how many emails you receive and the different types of emails you receive. My email now goes directly to labeled folders so that I know what to focus on first and have batches of lower priorities to work through when I'm able. If something isn't pressing, I don't even need to see it or waste attention sorting it when my email system could do that for me.

It's a communication management strategy that automatically organizes my emails based on timeliness and the priorities of my system. Even if you don't yet have a sufficient volume of email to feel overwhelmed, you'll find your messages begin to multiply exponentially as your network grows. I recommend getting organized from the beginning so communications don't start slipping through the cracks as you continue to build connections.

For example, my inbox has a folder called "Charities." I'm on multiple charity boards, but I don't need to see those messages when I go into my inbox to work with clients. I want to ensure my client communications don't get lost in a jumble of promotional emails or donation campaigns. When I've blocked out time for charity work, I can go through that folder separately.

All About Timing

When it comes to follow-up, timing is critical. I send notes not only to people I've just met but also to those I haven't talked to in a long time. My CRM can tell me when our last contact was, and I might follow up with a handwritten note, an email, or a text.

There's no agenda; maybe they won't respond. Often, though, just saying hi to someone I haven't seen for a while will yield interesting conversations and opportunities. It opens a dialogue and puts me top of mind.

Kody Bateman's book *Promptings* talks about the power of prompting people by telling them you care about them or are thinking about them. They may or may not respond, but putting that energy into the world comes back in cool ways.

I use my CRM to systemize some of the touchpoints and milestones while also spontaneously sending cards based on posts I see on social media to celebrate particular events. As I move through the world, I'm always looking for clues and prompts that someone could use a pick-me-up or would like to hear from me. If they've gone to the trouble of posting about something important to them, then I like to show I noticed and care.

I've received some great feedback, sometimes long after the fact, about notes I've sent. For instance, the wife of my mentor, Mic Johnson, owned a meeting-planning business, which was hit hard by the COVID-19 lockdowns. In-person meetings went away entirely for a period of time. That business had been the family's livelihood, but it went from having the best year ever to generating no money. We'd previously taken a trip together to Colorado to unplug and had a wonderful time, so to get their minds off the business struggles, I sent them a note with many photos from that trip. It meant a lot to them, and thankfully, now their business is back to thriving. It feels good to get these responses to my gifts and notes, and it shows me that they matter to the recipients. They receive my intended message: *I see you and hear you.*

Surprise and Delight: The Power of Gifting

Speaking of timing, when it's appropriate to send a gift will vary; stay attuned to the relationship you've developed and send something when you feel it will be authentic and not come off as overly sales-y. Understanding the difference takes practice and discernment. Usually, you want to interact with someone more than once before advancing to this stage. Whatever you send should reflect the curiosity you've shown and what you've learned about them rather than promoting your own agenda.

When deciding the timing of gifts, it's easiest to celebrate milestones. For instance, I love sending gifts to established clients when they experience big life moments like having a baby. At my firm, we often pick an item off the registry and send it along with a personalized piggy bank that has our logo on it. Sometimes, we later receive pictures of kids holding the piggy banks, which they enjoy shaking like maracas.

Our team has a shared document of gift ideas for different occasions. One of my favorites is a leather-bound journal with a subtle embossed logo. If people use it to write notes or take to networking meetings, they'll think of us. We also have champagne flutes delivered to clients' houses for anniversaries. If someone passes away, we like to name a star in their memory and give the naming certificate to the person grieving.

When someone I want to meet with isn't responding, sometimes I'll be a little cheeky and send a coffee gift card with a note that says, "Let's meet for coffee." It's a more confident, direct approach, but it works. If you put yourself out there, the worst a person can say is no—and one of my mottos is if you don't ask, the answer is always no. Don't be sales-y, but don't be afraid to ask.

To choose meaningful gifts, I pay attention to what people enjoy and then set reminders for myself to acknowledge those interests later. For instance, if we connect over a love of international travel, then I might make a note to bring them back a souvenir from my next trip. I've given personalized money belts to people who are planning for a big overseas adventure, a gift that is both useful and meaningful to them.

The key here is not just giving someone a gift but systematizing the reminder to get a meaningful gift in a future context that relates to your points of connection. Set those reminders right away because you can't remember everything. If you want this approach to work, you can't rely on your brain alone. Instead, create a timeline and refer back to it.

Systematizing Surprise

The CRM, timeline, and calendar reminders are systems for remembering and communicating, but there's also an element of trusting your intuition. Keep your ears pricked for details about what's going on in the person's life to generate gift ideas or at least content for your notes. Notice how you feel in someone's presence, how easy and genuine the conversation feels, what seems important to them, and then proceed accordingly. Not every interaction warrants a gift; trust yourself and use your judgment when you want to make a gesture that surprises and delights someone.

When planning to surprise people, set a budget. It costs money to send gifts. Because gifting is integral to my values and my system, I set aside part of my budget specifically for gift-giving. That way, I'm not going into debt or worrying about the cost. I've already accounted for it and can fit the gifts to the funds available. I also budget to support my friends' and contacts' charitable efforts. If I see someone raising money for charity on Facebook, I can donate twenty-five or one hundred dollars without second-guessing myself.

The more you can preplan and automate how you execute living One for All, the more it will become second nature. For instance, I also have notecards, pens, and stamps so that I can send a note when needed. If I'm in my car or traveling, I don't have to think, *Well, I would send a note if I had one.* I'm just already set up. Make everything as easy as possible, and remember that, ideally, you want to surprise and delight people in the love language they'll appreciate most. Notes often speak to people whose language is words of affirmation.

Personally, my love language is acts of service. Early on in dating, my wife learned that I don't need a gift, but I greatly appreciate having my dry cleaning picked up or my car washed. If you learn that someone else appreciates that same love language, then you can figure out favors for them that will be meaningful.

Part of systematizing active listening, which we discussed in Step Three, is staying attuned to clues about how people want to be appreciated. Instead of gifts or notes, some people want quality time, which might look like inviting them to a happy hour. That setting is less business-oriented and often gets them to open up and show a different side of themselves. If they don't drink, maybe the invitation is for a group dinner or to attend a Rotary meeting. There are multiple ways to offer your time.

Strategies for Resource Matching

There's an opportunity to add value in every situation, which is one of the real keys to living One for All. The key is finding it and then giving support, which often also leads to getting support in return.

For instance, I've been meeting a lot of people in startup businesses lately. I intuitively know some resources, and I've also intentionally sought out more. One contact recently left a successful company and moved his family from Kansas to Austin, Texas, to start his own business. I introduced him to someone who introduced him to someone else, who happened to connect him to a program called Launch Casey that gives grants to entrepreneurs. He won a grant for $55,000. Now he's happy and funded, and he has a new friendship with the person to whom I introduced him. He gives me credit, even though I didn't do anything except make the introduction. I simply like connecting people who have business ideas with helpful resources.

Resource matching isn't always as obvious as talking to someone in the startup space and knowing someone else in that industry to introduce them to. It could be hearing someone mention that they're expecting a new baby and knowing a nanny you could recommend, which has nothing to do with your professional background or the reason you're meeting. You're just listening for needs and finding ways to help in the broadest sense. Be open to the possibilities. The more people you know, the more likely you'll have a resource to offer.

You might think you don't know anyone, but when you think about all the different acquaintances and professionals you've met in any context (think back to Step Two), you'll start to realize that you already have resources to connect people with. Gradually expanding that network doesn't have to be overwhelming, and it can build your confidence to have more and more connections and options at your fingertips. You might be surprised at your capacity to resource match, even if it's not in the traditional way.

Behavioral Blueprints for Better Relationships

One follow-up tool I've found especially helpful is the Predictive Index (PI), a behavioral assessment that offers insight into how

ESSENTIAL PRINCIPLES FOR FOLLOWING UP

people think, communicate, and make decisions. For those unfamiliar, the PI measures four core behavioral drives—dominance, extraversion, patience, and formality—to create a unique profile of how someone prefers to work and interact. I like to send the assessment to new contacts after we've built a bit of rapport, not as a test but as a mutual discovery tool. The results often spark great conversations and give me a better sense of how to connect with and support that person going forward. Whether it's understanding how they like to be communicated with or what energizes them in a team environment, the PI helps me tailor my approach in a way that respects their individuality. It's one more way to deepen the relationship and move from surface-level networking to something much more meaningful.

One of the most powerful ways to follow through with intention is by understanding how you naturally operate and how others do, too. According to the Predictive Index, I'm a "captain," which means I'm a confident, intuitive self-starter who thrives on challenge, innovation, and making meaningful connections. I tend to move fast, communicate directly, and focus on getting results, but I've also learned that not everyone processes the world the same way I do. Knowing my PI profile helps me slow down, listen better, and flex my style to meet others where they are. That's what real connection is about.

I encourage you to take the Predictive Index yourself. It's not about putting yourself in a box; it's about unlocking a deeper understanding of how you show up in the world. When you know yourself better, you can be more intentional in how you support others. Whether you're a quiet problem-solver or a collaborative cheerleader, there's power in owning your style and using it to serve others more effectively.

It's interesting to note that when I took a similar assessment years ago, my results showed I would never thrive in sales. I didn't take that as a discouragement; instead, I used it as a discovery tool, a way to point out areas for growth, and a way to generate dialogue openers with others. The point here is not to overanalyze ourselves or one another. It's to be thoughtful about how we connect and engage.

Reciprocity

Give support, and you'll get support. That said, don't help people with the expectation of a direct or immediate reward. As you pour everything you have into the people you know, over time, the best candidates for deeper friendship, mutual interest, and engagement will rise to the top. Those are the ones you want to focus on. It's OK that not everyone will connect with and appreciate you as much as those core friends because you can't have a hundred best friends. Let the less engaged people be a more distant circle in the ecosystem of your connections. You don't need to cut them out, but you naturally won't invest as much in those relationships.

When you center service in your life, reciprocity happens all the time. Recently, when my dad was struggling with cancer, some connections surprised us with premade Kitch Meals, which was a huge help because it gave us one less thing to worry about.

I have experienced hundreds of these tiny moments of reciprocal compassion and service like this one, and I haven't forgotten a single one.

ACTION STEP

Personalize Your Communication Timeline

Over time, you will build your own detailed template to work from when you follow up with connections so that you don't have to reinvent the wheel every time. As you have more meetings, you'll start to see patterns in the topics you discuss while also crystallizing your personal brand. As you figure out what generally works and doesn't work, you can adapt your email template. Finding the winning formula doesn't happen overnight, but I'll give you a rundown of what mine includes so that you can start building and customizing your own.

It was great to meet you. I just wanted to follow up. I enjoyed learning [personal detail about them that you remember] *and hearing more about your background.* [Say more about whatever they shared thinking about, working on, experiencing with their family, and so on.]

Always mention something personal in the very beginning that is specific to the recipient so that it doesn't sound like a hollow form letter.

Here's a summary of the items we discussed:

- *We talked about life coaching; you can learn more about my life coach at* searcyfinancial.com/blog.
- *I'd love to invite you to Rotary, and I have a blog series about volunteering at* searcyfinancial.com/blog.
- [Fill in with bullets as applicable]

Here are some people from my network whom you might want to follow or connect with on LinkedIn:

- [Include bullets of the most relevant contacts with links to LinkedIn profiles]

Please let me know if I missed anything. If there's anything I can do to help you, I'm here. I look forward to a continued dialogue about how we can serve as resources for each other and our contacts. I appreciate you connecting me with people who share my interests, much like [Name of Introducer] *did when connecting us.*

My goal in sharing these resources is to ensure no meeting ever results in a dead end. People can go as deep as they want, but they'll always have more to explore, potentially strengthening ways we're connected through our common goals and interests.

Particularly when you're starting out, show your template to your mentors and ask for their feedback. How would the message strike them if they received it? What could you add, change, or strengthen to make it even more effective?

STEP FIVE
Nurture the Relationship

If you are really great, you will let others discover this fact from your actions.
—NAPOLEON HILL

Success often wears a deceptive mask. Just a few years ago, while everything appeared pristine on the surface, I was quietly drowning beneath the weight of compounding pressures. The convergence of personal and professional challenges—preparing for my son's arrival through out-of-state IVF treatments during the pandemic, supporting my wife in her role as health department director, serving on multiple nonprofit boards, being present for my mother's cancer battle, and navigating the purchase of my business—created a perfect storm of anxiety.

The manifestations were subtle at first: sleepless nights, vanishing appetite, and a growing resentment toward work as it competed with personal obligations. I lost thirty pounds and withdrew from social connections, a retreat made easier by COVID-19's imposed isolation. Though my network of mentors remained available, I struggled to reach out, carrying my burdens in silence. Even when I sought medical help and received a prescription for Lexapro, anxiety about taking anxiety medication only amplified my struggles.

This chapter, though it lasted only six months, taught me invaluable lessons about the importance of regular self-assessment. As 2021 transformed into 2022, external circumstances improved: the business purchase concluded, my mother's cancer subsided, and we welcomed our healthy son, Grant. Yet these victories highlighted how I'd been so focused on reaching destinations that I'd forgotten to embrace the journey.

The experience reshaped my approach to both personal and professional life and crystallized in several truths:

- "When everything is a priority, nothing is a priority."
- "You can't pour from an empty cup."
- "Be kind, for everyone you meet is fighting a hard battle."

While my struggles might seem modest to some, they were my battle, and they taught me perhaps the most crucial lesson of all: "The difference between successful people and very successful people is that very successful people say no to almost everything."

Today, I'm more proactive in recognizing unhealthy patterns, more open with my team about struggles, and more committed to maintaining balance. This vigilance serves two essential purposes: ensuring I can truly enjoy the journey and preserving the capacity to say yes to what matters most. In the end, the ability to set boundaries isn't just about preventing burnout—it's about creating space for life's most meaningful opportunities and moments.

In this final step of our journey, you'll find shared tips for nurturing the relationships you create through your one-on-one connection meetings, as well as nurturing the most important relationship of all: the one with yourself.

Methods to Maintain Accountability and Support Systems

There isn't an exact science to nurturing connection that I know of, but there are best practices that have worked for me and my team. For example, without any particular agenda, I like to reach out and check on people through text messages when something reminds me of them or when I scroll through my messages and realize I haven't communicated with them in a long time. There's no request; I simply tell them what reminded me of them and say I'm thinking of them. Maybe they respond, and maybe they don't, but it's fun to keep those contacts going.

From an information and memory recall standpoint, I use Salesforce and my professional Outlook email address for both business and personal contacts. I don't keep the two separate. I simply use the systems available through my business because, for me, business is personal. I love Salesforce for its functionality; it allows me to tailor my fields, track touchpoints, automate workflows, and maintain timelines for both business and personal relationships. That said, Salesforce isn't inexpensive, and it's not for everyone.

That approach might not work for others. If I weren't an owner of the company, for instance, then I'd risk losing all the information

I've acquired over nineteen years if I left. In your situation, you might want to ensure that your database is separate from your work or at least backed up or transferable. In banking and real estate, for instance, it seems like there's quite a bit of movement among companies, and you don't want to lose anything in that process, particularly personal relationships. I plan to continue using this system for life, so I need to ensure I have a way to transfer all my data when I retire.

If you're not a company owner, find a way to set up a contact management system that also has the capabilities of timelines of tasks and reminders. Depending on the nature of your work, your personal and business contacts may end up being separate, but you need to systemize both. There are a number of personal CRM tools available today that are easy to use, independent of your employer's systems, and often free or low-cost. Here are a few personal CRM tools to consider at the time of this writing if you want to build your own system outside of your employer's platform:

- **HubSpot CRM.** Free, professional-grade CRM with strong integrations and reliable support. Great for business-minded users who want something that feels similar to Salesforce.
- **Clay.** Beautifully designed, AI-powered tool that helps you remember key personal details and prompts thoughtful follow-ups.
- **Dex.** Simple and effective, with great integration for LinkedIn and helpful reminders to stay in touch.
- **Covve.** Mobile-first, syncs with your phone, and helps auto-enrich contact data.
- **Monica.** Privacy-friendly, open-source CRM built for managing personal relationships, not just professional ones.

METHODS TO MAINTAIN ACCOUNTABILITY AND SUPPORT SYSTEMS

- **Folk.** A flexible option for freelancers and small teams who want to organize people by projects, roles, or industries.
- **Honorable Mentions:** Airtable (customizable), Notion (template-based), Contacts+ (supercharged phone book), and HiHello (digital business card app).

When you systemize, you can be more present with whatever's in front of you. The busier you are, the more present you need to be. Timelines and systems help you keep track of what you need to do or what you said you'd follow up on in two weeks, a month, or a year. The reminders need to align with a calendar, not just be a jumble of notes you keep having to reread and sort through.

We're creating efficiency here: it's not practical to reread everything every time you need a piece of information. If I don't need to follow up on something for a year, then I don't even want to think about it until it's time. If I know that a reminder will pop up at the proper interval to prompt me to prepare, then I can let it completely slip my mind until then without concern.

How and What to Delegate

If you're just starting out in your career, you probably don't have much opportunity to delegate. However, it's wise to figure out how to make your work delegable so that you have a system you can communicate to others when you reach that point. In my business, we create processes that anyone can follow. The information needs to live in an accessible place outside my head or the head of the person responsible for the task, whether it's creating a spreadsheet every week or researching stocks.

The more I can create replicable processes for tasks, the more time I can free up to do what can't be delegated: relationship building. For example, I might be able to delegate sending a follow-up note if I won't get to it otherwise (though I personally emphasize writing notes by hand and including information an assistant wouldn't know), but I can't delegate attending a personal coffee. Prioritize timeliness and delegate whatever you can so that you have maximal time for what only you can do. Process-driven work needs to be delegated once you reach a certain level of responsibility. For example, I delegate data entry to a human assistant. If I meet someone new or get a new introduction, I forward the contact information to her to input into the CRM. She can research and add where the person works, input any contact details from their signature line, list any referrals we've made for each other, and include where and when I met them in the CRM. If I make an introduction to them, I bcc my assistant so that she can add that information to Salesforce. That way, I have everything I need to continue a conversation if I don't see the person again for a year. There's no reason for me to personally spend time on that easily delegated task, but all that information is hugely useful later.

The bottom line? Use your energy wisely—which usually means using it on humans.

Show Up Intentionally on Social Media

One of the simplest and most scalable ways to nurture relationships today is through social media. I recommend choosing one or two platforms that feel authentic to you. For me, those are LinkedIn and Facebook. I've made it part of my daily rhythm to spend just a few minutes spreading positivity and engaging with others online.

This doesn't require creating viral content or becoming an influencer. It's about consistency and contribution. Like others' posts. Leave comments that add encouragement, insight, or ideas. Tag people, nonprofits, or organizations you care about when you share meaningful content. When you help amplify others, you're not just showing support—you're showing up.

Over time, this kind of thoughtful interaction helps position you as a connector and thought leader, even if that's not your goal. Research continues to show that active participation on social platforms improves visibility, relevance, and connection. It also helps the algorithm surface you to others you may not know yet—but probably should.

Make sure your Connection Piece (the one we discussed in Step One) is easy to find on your profile for each platform you use. Consider pinning it to the top of your profile or keeping it handy in your About or Featured sections. Then use the topics or causes from your Connection Piece to guide your posts. It'll keep your sharing aligned with your values—and help attract others who care about the same things.

In my opinion, the most important part of showing up on social media is consistency. This can't be something you do once in a while and expect results. It's best to build it into your daily life. Just a few minutes a day can have a compounding effect—on your visibility, your relationships, and the energy you put into the world.

While there's often a lot of negativity in the news around social media, I choose to find the positive. I've seen it bring people together, reconnect old friends, launch meaningful projects, and spread kindness across communities. That's the version of social media I want to be part of—and I encourage you to do the same.

Try Communication That Transcends Business

In addition to leveraging social media, consider ways to nurture your relationships that are not related to work (or work-adjacent), too. My company newsletter, for instance, includes coverage of our community service, which is sometimes why people want to do business with us in the first place. It's an automated way to stay in front of people with good content, which is important. When I meet someone new, I tell them I'm going to add them to the newsletter unless they request otherwise. That way, I grow the subscriber list but don't surprise anyone or add people before we've made a personal connection. Some people might find that pushy, but I make it clear they can opt out with no hard feelings.

The newsletter goes out to more than two thousand people, but it feels personal because I always introduce it with a message about what's been going on in my life. Because I include that information, people respond with their thoughts on particular articles or tell me what they've been up to in return. It's a systemized way to keep in touch.

Take care on timing: you don't want to seem like you're spamming people or have them tune you out, so don't overdo it. I only send our newsletter every other month; you may choose a different cadence for your communication, but the point is to be mindful of how (and how frequently) your message will be received. Focus on quality over quantity.

If you choose to use a newsletter to stay in touch and nurture relationships, pay attention to who is in your audience and what your goals are for the newsletter. Be intentional based on your industry, your connections, your values, and your vision for your community. Don't inundate people with content they're unlikely to read, enjoy, or act on, as they'll be more likely to unsubscribe and tune you out. Be yourself, and include aspects of your personal life that will foster connection, such as your family, travel, or hobbies. In my experience, including your human side emphasizes the relationship aspect of business much better than a stuffy update that only focuses on professional concerns.

Know When to Let a Relationship Go

Living One for All and systemizing kindness emphasizes nurturing relationships in a systematic way, but you can't reasonably nurture every relationship the same. You can't be all things to all people. So, sometimes, you need to compartmentalize or make decisions about what and whom to prioritize.

When connecting with new people, there's a lot of activity at the beginning. How much you invest into following up with the timeline depends on the relationship. If I want to stick with someone, I find a way to meet with them again in a few months, and I set myself a reminder to follow up. If someone gets my follow-up email, receives my introductions, and gets added to my newsletter but doesn't show potential for mutual engagement after that, then I don't need to set myself a reminder to do anything else. If they want to follow up with me, they can.

Sometimes, if I haven't heard back from someone after offering to make introductions or help in some way, I'll send a final follow-up note that gives them an easy out. I might write something like, "Unless I hear differently from you, I'll assume you're not interested in the introductions at this time." It might sound a little bold or even passive-aggressive in writing, but it's actually a kindness—it gives them the chance to say no or clarify their situation. More often than not, I'll get a reply like, "Sorry! I've been underwater lately," or "I definitely want to connect—can we revisit in a few weeks?" Either way, I get clarity. And when they do respond, I simply update my notes and shift the follow-up timeline accordingly. Not everyone is as dialed in with follow-through as I am, and that's OK. This technique lets me keep the relationship door open while still honoring my time and boundaries.

How often you check in with someone will depend on the type of relationship, potential, and mutual sense of connection. When there doesn't seem to be much energy or potential in the connection, then you can either put off following up until you have a lull in your calendar or let it go entirely. Cultivating relationships comes without expectations; the only requirements are to be kind and to do anything you say you're going to do. So, if you're kind and helpful in your meetings and follow through with anything you've committed to, then it's OK if a connection runs its course.

The value you can provide or how you can meet the person's needs will determine the frequency of outreach, which might taper off as you go along. If you've done what you can do and they no longer follow up with you, that's OK. You'll naturally continue investing in relationships where you both move toward each other with interesting ideas, opportunities, or conversations. Reciprocal engagement doesn't necessarily mean the person spends money on your business, but if the relationship is one-sided and you're always trying to chase them down, it makes sense to turn your attention toward the more sustainable and mutual connections.

Sometimes, I get a thank-you email for sending a thank-you note. The recipient definitely didn't need to thank me, but doing so communicates that they're interested in the connection, too. If I send resources and someone is responsive, that's another sign of interest and mutuality. If I make an introduction but don't hear anything afterward, then they probably aren't as interested in continuing a conversation. I always try to deliver on what I say

I'll do, and I try to stay connected with people who share that value. The people who don't tend to recede from my circle over time, as they likely will from yours, too.

Your Biggest Relationship

Don't overlook the value of continuing to invest in your biggest relationship: the one with yourself.

Every year, I look for something to get involved with to expand my perspective and help me think in a different way, whether it's joining a group, getting help with a goal, or improving myself by another means. That approach is key to leadership development. For instance, I completed a year-long program through the Leaders Institute, meeting with thirty people every other month. I made some new friends, connected with leaders from different backgrounds, and learned new skills. I try to be hands-on because it's great to read a personal development book, but nothing changes unless you apply what you learn to other people. I also participate in the Pathway to Mastery every year. It focuses on realtors, but I gain new insights as a financial planner as well.

Whatever your goals and interests, find ways to invest in and nurture yourself. Healthy relationships require managing boundaries and devoting energy to what matters, which includes the internal work of self-improvement. Always be on the lookout for ways you can push yourself forward by learning something or meeting someone new.

Making that commitment requires pushing yourself out of your comfort zone. It's OK to be uncomfortable. Would you really feel satisfied if you retired at sixty-five and had never done anything difficult or uncomfortable your whole career? I know I'd feel regret in that situation. The thing about getting out of your comfort zone is after a while, the unfamiliar feels comfortable, which is your cue to stretch yet again. It's a never-ending process.

I've made mistakes in this approach. Earlier in my life, I said yes to literally everything, and it didn't serve me. As I've shared with you in this book, I didn't have time to meet a spouse, and I neglected my own personal satisfaction. I didn't have healthy boundaries. Today, I'm still doing just as much, but in a more intentional way and with a better team supporting me to do it. I've still experienced periods of overwhelm, but I've learned to prioritize, balance, delegate, and systemize.

When everything's a priority, nothing's a priority. It's important to commit to what aligns with your values, serves your goals, and is possible to achieve. One of my values is to follow through, so it doesn't serve me or the people I'm trying to help if I commit to something I can't actually deliver. I'm not perfect, and sometimes I still make mistakes. When I get out over my skis, I tend to throttle new connections and reduce what I agree to for a while until I can catch up.

For a while, I throttled new business at the firm because I didn't want to overwhelm my team. It takes time to put the processes and delegation in place to scale effectively, whether you're growing your business or expanding your personal connections. You need to grow in a way you can maintain because, otherwise, you'll drop too many balls, and you'll lose connections as fast as you make them. Be careful not to overextend yourself.

My business is all about long-term relationships. Other businesses might have a different model. If a realtor sells a house, that's the end of their contract with that client. In financial planning, by contrast, we aim to work with people for life.

I balance helping others with my commitment to personal growth by integrating the personal and professional. Every personal relationship is a business relationship because business is personal for me. As I've noted, Warren Buffett says the key to success is saying no to almost everything. To me, this looks like saying no to what doesn't align with your goals so that when the big yes comes, you have the bandwidth to jump on it.

There's nuance and maybe a little contradiction to this approach because I prize saying yes and helping everyone I can. However, I'm just one person with only twenty-four hours in the day, so I have to make choices. I say no to much more than I used to, which creates capacity for the big yeses. It helps to have a coach and mentors to hold me accountable and call me out when I get too busy and scattered.

Putting It All Together

At this point, you've learned the core system for systematizing kindness and living life One for All. You've started to identify or clarify what you want to be remembered for, your core purpose. You've discovered how you can help, starting with people who hunt in the same forest and expanding from there. You've identified people you can connect with in person and thought about how to leave them remembering that you made them feel good, valued, heard, respected, and helped. You understand that your brand is only as strong as your follow-through, and you have the tools to systemize your reminders rather than trying to do the impossible by remembering everything in your head. You know how to nurture your most important relationships, including the one with yourself so that you and your community can grow and thrive together.

The only thing left to do? Get out there and start supporting others like it's your job. I can't wait to hear about your journey of connection. Thank you for being a part of mine.

ACTION STEP

Turn Your Connection Piece into Shareable Content

As you continue to nurture relationships, consider creating content around the things that matter most to you. A great place to start is with the topics in your Connection Piece (introduced in Step One). These are the things you want to be remembered for: your values, your causes, your community, and your vision for how you can help.

Writing about them not only helps clarify your own message but also gives others a chance to engage more deeply with who you are and what you stand for.

For example, I've written a series of short blog posts called *Why I Volunteer*, which highlights the nonprofits I serve and why I care about them. When someone asks about my involvement with a nonprofit, I can simply send them the link. It's authentic, easy to share, and a helpful resource for those who might want to get involved too.

Another example? Because of my love for K-State University, I'm often asked, "What should I do, see, or eat when I'm in the Little Apple?" Instead of rewriting the same message each time, I created a piece called *Why I Love the Little Apple*. Now, I can share it with anyone in a few seconds, and it often sparks great conversations.

As you create content like this, don't underestimate the power of photos. Share images of you at the event, volunteering, traveling, or just being yourself. These photos give people, many of whom you may not have met yet, an opportunity to feel like they already know you. That familiarity builds trust before your first real interaction, which accelerates the relationship-building process and makes connecting even easier. People resonate with real faces and real stories.

The content you create can be about anything:

- A place you love
- A cause you support
- A way you help others
- A life lesson you've learned
- Or something you get asked about over and over again

Even if your business has nothing to do with that topic directly, sharing these personal insights helps build trust and credibility. You're showing people who you are and not just what you do. That kind of visibility deepens connections and reinforces the idea that people do business with people, not businesses.

Assuming your compliance rules allow it, I also recommend posting this content on your company website. That way, even if someone finds you while searching for something unrelated—say, a local nonprofit or tips about your hometown—they can still quickly learn what you do professionally and how you can help.

The bonus? This kind of content helps your SEO (search engine optimization), especially when it's tied to authentic topics you care about. It connects your name to your values and often leads to more meaningful relationship development.

If you're building a business where your team plays a vital role, make sure they understand this too. Help them see that their stories, interests, and relationships are part of what makes the company successful. When everyone is showing up in service of others, living One for All creates exponential results.

Conclusion

*The capacity to care is the thing which gives life
its deepest meaning and significance.*
—PABLO CASALS

I know what you must be thinking: *Ok, what now?* Great ideas are only effective if you put them into action. Before you close this book, I want you to take a few moments to inventory where you are, where you want to go, and what the next right step is to get there.

Do you have a mentor to help you grow your community and career, or do you need to find one? If you need to find one, who will you email, call, or text by tomorrow afternoon to move that process forward? Remember: if you don't ask, the answer is always no.

No matter where you are in the process, there's a manageable, near-term action you can take to keep moving forward. For prompts, checklists, and suggested solutions, I invite you to visit searcyfinancial.com/OneforAll, which offers an updated list of resources to help you get your bearings. There's also a list of recommended reading in the backmatter of this book.

Remember: whatever we do, we'll perpetuate a cycle; it's up to you whether you engage in a virtuous one or a negative one. You can look for the good in people, the abundance in the world, and how you can help—or you can do the opposite.

If you made it to the end of this book, I feel confident about which option you'll choose.

As you continue on this journey, I hope you'll apply the lens of systematizing to every positive step you take. Random acts of kindness are nice, but they're not replicable and reliable. Living One for All is more than random. Now that you know the ingredients that truly help others, build communities, improve the world, and come back around to enrich your own life, how can you infuse them into every day and everything you do?

I'd love to hear how you run with this system and make it your own. Please share your learning moments and success stories with me on LinkedIn and Facebook (it's my real name, so I'll be easy to find). If you'd like to stay in touch, you can subscribe to my newsletter at searcyfinancial.com/OneforAll.

I hope this book has helped you, and I can't wait to see how you contribute to the growing community of people committed to living One for All!

Acknowledgments

To my family. Thank you for your unwavering support and encouragement as I committed to writing this book. Your belief in me made all the difference.

To the mentors, both seasoned and new, who've poured wisdom into my journey. Thank you. Your guidance has shaped my growth and direction more than you'll ever know.

To the incredible team at Searcy Financial Services. Thank you for making it possible for me to live out my purpose every day. Your dedication ensures our firm thrives, even while I chase down creative side projects like this one.

To those who challenged me to write a book, even though writing wasn't always a strength. Thank you. Your push helped me discover a new joy, and this won't be the last time I put pen to paper.

To my clients. Thank you for trusting me with so much more than financial planning. It's been my life's work to ensure that all we touch is better because of something we did. That purpose is alive and well in our firm culture.

To Mike Searcy. Thank you for laying the foundation of this firm with a servant's heart. You've pushed me into challenges I once thought I couldn't handle, and that's exactly what helped me grow.

To my life coach. Thank you for helping me break out of my comfort zone and lean into new possibilities faster than I ever thought possible.

And finally, to God. Thank you for the grace, the growth, and the people who've shaped this journey.

Recommended Reading

You'll be the same person in five years except for the people you meet and the books you read.
—CHARLIE "TREMENDOUS" JONES

Personal Development
- *The Monk Who Sold His Ferrari* by Robin Sharma
- *Atomic Habits* by James Clear
- *High Performance Habits* by Brendon Burchard
- *The Power of One More* by Ed Mylett
- *Four Thousand Weeks* by Oliver Burkeman
- *The Top Five Regrets of the Dying* by Bronnie Ware
- *The Untethered Soul* by Michael A. Singer
- *Man's Search for Meaning* by Viktor Frankl

Business & Sales
- *Fanatical Prospecting* by Jeb Blount
- *The Greatest Salesman in the World* by Og Mandino
- *Selling from the Heart* by Larry Levine
- *Be Obsessed or Be Average* by Grant Cardone
- *Who Not How* by Dan Sullivan
- *10x is Easier Than 2x* by Dan Sullivan
- *Unreasonable Hospitality: The Remarkable Power of Giving People More Than They Expect* by Will Guidara

- *Scripts* by Nick Murray
- *Start with Why* by Simon Sinek
- *To Sell Is Human* by Daniel H. Pink

Financial Wisdom
- *Die with Zero* by Bill Perkins
- *The One Page Financial Plan* by Carl Richards
- *Money Isn't the Problem, You Are* by Gary Douglas and Dain Heer
- *Killing Sacred Cows* by Garrett Gunderson
- *The Behavior Gap* by Carl Richards
- *The Five Types of Wealth* by Sahil Bloom

Leadership & Success
- *Think and Grow Rich* by Napoleon Hill
- *More Than a Season* by Dayton Moore
- *All It Takes is a Goal* by Jon Acuff
- *The 12 Week Year* by Brian Moran and Michael Lennington
- *Reality-Based Leadership* by Cy Wakeman
- *Leaders Eat Last* by Simon Sinek
- *Buy Back Your Time* by Dan Martell

Relationship Building
- *Giftology* by John Ruhlin
- *The Power of Human Connection* by Kody Bateman
- *Promptings* by Kody Bateman
- *Give and Take* by Adam Grant
- *Sharpen* by Dan Cooper and Drew Hiss
- *Authentic Relating: A Guide to Rich, Meaningful, Nourishing Relationships* by Ryel Kestano

Recommended Reading

Kansas City Authors
- *Reflections at The Crossroads—A Personal Journey of Ambition and Authenticity* by Ken Bramble
- *You Might be an Asshole: But It Might Not Be Your Fault* by Dr. Katie Ervin
- *Closing the Trust Gap: Taking Action on What Matters Most* by Cory Scheer
- *The Purposeful Growth Revolution* by Mark Mears
- *The High Achiever's Guide* by Maki Moussavi
- *Small Ball Big Dreams* by Joel Goldberg
- *Get-Real Leadership: A Practical Approach That Delivers Relationships, Respect and Results* by Harry Campbell
- *Get-Real Culture: A Practical Approach to Creating a Wildly Successful Workplace* by Harry Campbell
- *Get-Real Mindset: A Practical Approach to Winning at the Margin* by Harry Campbell
- *Embrace Your Freakness* by Frank Keck

For Advisors
- *Succession Planning for Financial Advisors—Building an Enduring Business* by David Grau Sr.
- *Building with the End in Mind* by David Grau Sr.
- *Scripts* by Nick Murray
- *The Behavior Gap* by Carl Richards
- *The Ensemble Practice: A Team-Based Approach to Building a Superior Wealth Management Firm* by Philip Palaveev

About the Author

Marc C. Shaffer, CFP®, AIF®, EA is a financial planner, business owner, and relationship-builder who believes that kindness isn't just a virtue—it's a strategy. As a partner at Searcy Financial Services, he specializes in helping individuals and families align their wealth with their values and create intentional legacies that span generations.

Marc holds a degree in Personal Financial Planning from Kansas State University and was honored as a 2023 Alumni Fellow for the K-State College of Health and Human Sciences. He has served in leadership roles for numerous community and university boards, including the Overland Park South Rotary Club, Growing Futures Early Education, and the Wabash CannonBall Steering Committee, which raises scholarship funds for future Wildcats.

Marc lives in Overland Park, Kansas, with his wife, Bridgette, and their children, Grant and Emily. An avid traveler and outdoor enthusiast, Marc has completed multi-day hikes in places like Patagonia, Peru, Iceland, Bhutan, and beyond—experiences that continue to shape his perspective on connection, generosity, and purposeful living.

The system he shares in this book reflects the heart of how he lives, leads, and builds lasting relationships—with clients, community, and the people he serves every day.

www.ingramcontent.com/pod-product-compliance
Lightning Source LLC
Chambersburg PA
CBHW070632030426
42337CB00020B/3989